In Praise of Stay-at-Home Moms

In Praise of Stay-at-Home Moms

Dr. Laura Schlessinger

HARPER LUXE

An Imprint of HarperCollins*Publishers*

HarperCollins books may be purchased for educational, business, or sales promotional use. For information please write: Special Markets Department, HarperCollins Publishers, 10 East 53rd Street, New York, NY 10022.

FIRST HARPERLUXE EDITION

HarperLuxe™ is a trademark of HarperCollins Publishers

Library of Congress Cataloging-in-Publication Data is available upon request.

ISBN: 978-0-06-172011-6

09 10 11 12 13 ID/RRD 10 9 8 7 6 5 4 3 2 1

Contents

Preface

With appropriate apologies to Shakespeare, I come to praise at-home moms, not to bury full-time working moms. This is not another missile attack in the "mommy wars," nor is it a debate on day care versus mommy care. This is also not a treatise on the benefits to children of being with a loving parent rather than with hired help or in an institutionalized group care setting. I will leave these arguments to wiser folks than I, and statistics and research results are generally appreciated only by those who wish to feel convinced or vindicated by them.

I will admit to being surprised—no, amazed—that a whole generation and a half of women have been so easily enraptured by the suggestion that what they have to give their child is easily replaced by a nanny, babysitter, or day-care worker. A baby is conceived in a woman's body, is nurtured there for nine months, and then suckles at her breast, more aware of her voice than anyone else's in the universe—and then her arms, kisses, laughs, tickles, warmth, coos, and so forth can be substituted for with a routine of feeding, diapering, and snacks? Well, since so many people say it is so, I guess it must be so; therefore, no argument from me.

I am personally moved by and interested in the lovely stories of warmth, love, and sacrifice told by families who've structured themselves to focus on enjoying every possible moment of their child's journey in development—and I'm sure there are equivalent emotional highs from watching one's child's journey via nanny cam and day-care worker daily reports.

I would never dream of telling a woman what she should do to make her life fulfilling, exciting, and purposeful. There are, of course, many ways to achieve personal satisfaction. I would never dream of telling a woman that she is needed more by her family than anywhere else on the planet, because I wouldn't want her to suffer any guilt or sense of loss if she chose to be in a full-time career. I would never dream of telling a woman that the special sweetness and nurturance that only a woman can bring to a home might bring her a depth of joy and peace that she never imagined, because I might seem offensive to those women who don't—and I certainly don't wish to offend anybody.

No, I am not here to condemn anyone for anything; I am here only to let you know of the lives of families with at-home moms. I hope you will be touched, tickled, moved, and entertained by what follows.

INTRODUCTION

Until I was thirty-five, I never wanted to be a mother. At least, that's what I thought, largely because of having been in university during the 1960s, when I was brainwashed (aka had my consciousness raised) into being a feminista for whom a career, with its promise of personal importance, power, and success, was what a real woman was supposed to aspire to. I knew for sure that I was definitely not going to become like my perpetually angry, frustrated mother, who always behaved as though being a wife and mother were tantamount to self-immolation even though neither my dad nor circumstances ever kept her from doing anything she wanted to do.

Nope, no *Little House on the Prairie* beginnings for me.

The problem was, no matter how many successes I had, there was that constant "something missing" feeling. It didn't dawn on me that the empty feeling had to do with my uterus, breasts, and arms; I was clearly missing being a mommy. I woke up to that fact while watching a PBS *NOVA* presentation on the miracle of life. Using fiber optics, they showed sperm swimming up through a woman's cervix into the uterus, where they made their way into the fallopian tube to meet the egg newly ejected by the ovary. The moment of fertilization was recorded, as was the embryo's trip down into the uterus to implant in the wall and continue development. The magical miracle of the whole subsequent nine months of gestation was condensed into sixty incredible minutes. The final scene was the baby born vaginally and placed naked, wet, and surprised onto the mother's belly while Mom and Dad cooed and whooped.

By the tears on my face and the ache in my chest, I had found clarity as to what was missing. After a marriage, many infertility treatments, monthly disappointments, and one tubal pregnancy later, finally my quest ended in an emergency C-section wherein a nine-pound son was delivered from his petite mom—and our lives were never the same again.

The first three months were hell—sleep deprivation and a constantly crying baby made me wonder what

I had been thinking! My husband kept reminding me that this phase isn't permanent, but it was difficult to believe him. And then one day, exactly three months to the minute after his birth, our son slept through the night.

As my mother had chosen to abandon both her then adult daughters, I had no motherly advice or assistance. It doesn't matter how book-learned you are about children and parenting; when you're postpartum, all intellect evaporates and you're simply an emotional heap of worry, self-doubt, confusion, fear, and exhaustion. The other problem for me was recovering from the C-section. We did hire a "motherly" woman for two weeks to come in and show me how to handle things. She was a godsend.

In the years before my son started kindergarten, we did try two preschool-like establishments to see if they had any benefit for him. One of them lasted one day. When I came at 4:00 PM to find that he hadn't stopped crying, that was the end of that. The headmistress gave me the usual argument that he needed to adjust, but I saw no reason to torture my child with my absence until he accepted his loss. The second time was when we were financially desperate, and I needed to do some part-time radio fill-in for some extra money to survive. At first he liked the experience, but after a few weeks the routine became boring, and he yearned to be with me, doing all the stuff we'd do in a day: playing, reading, errands, dancing, artwork, words and spelling, cycling, hiking, and so forth. So that was the end of that.

I am grateful for every moment I've had as a mommy. I have great memories of twirling my son around in a shopping cart in a local Target store's parking lot (a lot cheaper than Magic Mountain), or of us walking through a forest, pretending that we were being tracked by monsters, selecting sticks for swords and spears, and working together to get to safety. Now he's a paratrooper in the U.S. Army!

My husband and I came to the practical conclusion that I needed to go back to radio work to be our family's primary financial support, while he would manage my career, the home, and our finances. Nonetheless, I refused to take any job that would require me to be out of the home every day while our son was home or awake! I would take care of him all day and then go to work on radio, leaving the house at 9:00 PM after putting him to bed. Eventually, when he started kindergarten, I landed a daytime shift while he was in school.

In order to do the writing and necessary research, I would get up at 5:00 AM and work a few hours before I woke him up to get ready for school. I always worked my career around my family, never the other way around.

The first book I published, *Ten Stupid Things Women Do to Mess Up Their Lives*, required me to travel up and down the West Coast for interviews. I got all my son's teachers to give me his work for the week and took him with me. He did his work and had a blast traveling, meeting people, and keeping me company. He did cost my publisher a pretty penny, eating all the goodies in the minibar. Then I found out about satellite interviews; I could do twenty-five local and national television shows in one early-morning session, I discovered, so I didn't have to leave home to promote my book.

I have been attacked incessantly for supposed hypocrisy concerning this issue of child care; I couldn't possibly have done all the things required of my career without neglecting my son, the argument goes. Well, those critics are just plain wrong—and clearly defensive out of some well-earned guilt. It is so very doable if you are:

- committed to the priority of raising your children yourself;

- part of a marriage, which obviously provides two parents;

- willing to sacrifice some opportunities for the sake of family;

- willing to "do without" many things—but not family time and attention; and

- not willing to compromise on your conviction, no matter how pressed you get by circumstances or naysayers.

None of these efforts, I should say, guarantees that your kids will never be a pain in the butt or get into stupid situations. I will say, however, that your children are less likely to be major pains in the butt or to get into horrendous situations. The closer the family and the more hands-on time spent with children, the more likely those children—as impulsive and impetuous as they normally are—will set some limits on their youthful experimentation and nonsense.

Of course, it is also possible for a child brought up mostly in day care, or by nannies and/or babysitters, to be successful, personally and professionally. I wouldn't dream of suggesting that there are any real benefits to children from having at-home parents; it's just a choice, like French or vinaigrette dressing on your salad. Isn't it? Well, sure that's right, because if you knew you were going to be recycled and come back as an infant with a choice, you'd choose a mommy, a nanny, a babysitter, or a day-care worker for yourself with equal enthusiasm—right?

There used to be a guilt factor about parenting your own kids versus paying someone else to. Guilt is not the motivator it used to be, as folks have shifted from "should" to "feel like/or not." These days, the "feely" answer usually wins out. The freedom from responsibilities that don't lend immediate gratification, compensation, or glorification may be a surprise freedom from having deep meaning in one's life . . . but you can't have everything.

During 2007 a spate of überfeminist authors laid guilt on women who didn't abandon their children to "other care," lest they do the universe and their children actual harm (no, I'm not kidding or exaggerating) by staying home with them. All the morning television talk shows glorified, in a largely one-sided manner, of course, the necessary course of action for a woman to avoid wasting herself in the mire of her children's needs and her husband's desires.

That's when the feminist movement's mantra of choice got confusing: the decision to be a homemaker and full-time mother became a stupid, gross, dangerous error instead of a respected opportunity for self-expression and a deeper valuing of family life with regard to the well-being of a woman.

However, in all fairness, that's why it is called "the women's movement"—it is for, by, and about the well-being of women, not children or families. Wait, don't women benefit from the joy of motherhood and the bonding of marriage? I guess feminism does not see those as significant enough to warrant making the sacrifices necessary for the commitment to child-rearing and wife-ing. I get so confused.

I recently received an e-mail from a young girl doing a pro-con report for school on day care versus mother care. She wanted me to give her information, as arguments in favor of the mother-care side seemed difficult to find. What research could I give her that would not be vulnerable to dispute? I pondered that question for an entire morning.

The answer came in the form of an e-mail that arrived just before I turned on my microphone to do my daily radio show:

> *As I sit to write this letter, my hope is that if just one mother can hear what I have to say and holds her child just a little tighter today, I will have fulfilled my reason for writing.*
>
> *By the time I was 29 our family was complete. I had three beautiful children, a loving husband, and although never money to spare, we found ways to get by. I had stopped working full-time and started part-time shortly after my first child was born*

because I loved being with her. Although I had my mother and mother-in-law to babysit whenever I needed, by the time my middle son was born, I knew I could not work anymore. Something inside of me told me that I had to spend as much time with my children as I could. My husband worked extra hours, I made do with what we had, and we made things work for us. My husband would work at night or at home, but if there was a baseball game—he was there. I cut everyone's hair, including my own, did my own nails, and never bought anything that was not on sale. We were happy.

There were many days where I was pulling out my hair, found myself screaming at them, and was totally exhausted by the end of the day, thinking to myself, "Any other work would be a pleasant relief." But there were also many moments I would never trade in for any job, no matter what the pay. Those moments when your child gives you a smile or a look you never forget, moments when they would give you a kiss, a hug, or just hold your hand for no reason. Those are the moments a mother treasures in her heart forever and they can never be replaced, not even by a grandmother.

I was selfish—I wanted my children to know me, and I wanted to be that special person in their lives.

Although I didn't know it then, and on certain days may have told you otherwise, my life was perfect.

Maybe life isn't meant to be lived perfectly. Perhaps I took too many things for granted. But our life is no longer that perfect storybook tale. Two years ago my middle son was killed in an auto accident. He was 22 years old. He was away at college when he decided to get in a car where the driver had been drinking; ten minutes later he was dead.

Our lives will never be the same again; the world as we knew it has been destroyed. We miss our son terribly. My husband, surviving two children, and I will never be the same, but we are trying to hold on to each other and pick up the pieces, one piece at a time.

Dr. Laura, there is only one thing I can say. I am so grateful for those moments I had with my son. Those moments, the good as well as the crazy ones, I will forever hold close to my heart. All those precious years I spent with my son now are what help me get through the day.

So please, Dr. Laura, never stop preaching to all the young moms who feel they can't handle it, are struggling with making it through the day, who believe they "need" to work instead of being with their child, just how much it might someday mean to them to have spent those precious moments with their children. Hopefully other moms can just take my word for it: Don't let anyone or anything prevent you from holding them, hugging them, playing with them, memorizing their smile, their laughter, their heart.

Our children are such special gifts that should never be taken for granted, and life is so unpredictable, we never know if today we will breathe our last breath.

—Lisa

As obviously touching and compelling as Lisa's letter is, I'm sure the überfeminists would recommend that the touching alternative would be to stockpile reports and videos taken by day-care workers, nannies, and babysitters, so that if the worst does happen, and a child is lost, you still have those memories . . . just through the eyes of other people.

Close enough?

This book is dedicated to the praise of at-home moms; from one mommy to so many others.

Affectionately,

Dr. Laura C. Schlessinger
"I am my kid's mom"

1

THE DECISION

There was a time, long ago, when parents agonized over the sad necessity of finding some sort of child care due to deaths, financial disasters, and other catastrophes. Under these conditions families often struggled with feelings of failure, guilt, and loss at having to outsource the warmth of parenting to hired help.

The "greatest generation" isn't limited to those folks who served valiantly at war; it embraces the folks who worked on the farms and in the factories, toiling at difficult jobs to not only serve their country but provide for their families. Little mentioned are the women who birthed their babies, raised their kids, and managed the home and the budget so that there would be food in the family's tummies and clothes on their backs, taught their children right from wrong, and made sure they washed behind their ears and got to school on time. In those days there was very little bellyaching about "finding yourself," "time for me," or "what is my identity?"; women were respected for their commitments and talents, and in spite of hardships, they felt important to their families and communities.

Just in case you think this is all anachronistic, contemplate this recent letter from a listener:

> As I've been thinking and listening to your show, I've realized that our terminology surrounding women who choose to stay at home with their families has changed. We've become "stay-at-home moms" or, often negatively, "housewives," rather than "homemakers." My suspicion is that women have coined themselves SAHMs because they're wanting to be competitive with their "working mother" counterparts (as if staying at home isn't working!).
>
> Perhaps we've believed the lie that being a "homemaker" is old-fashioned and therefore irrelevant. However, I have come to realize that though my primary motivation for spending my days in my home is in fact taking care of my children, I do much more than that. I spend my days making a home, not just for my children, but for my husband and myself.

Cleaning and organizing, playing with and teaching my children, shopping and running errands, taking care of finances, doing laundry, taking care of doctor appointments, communicating with teachers, organizing the family calendar, cooking meals, and making our home a comfortable, cozy, and welcoming place for us and our extended family and friends, among other things, is not just being a "stay-at-home mom." I am making a house a home, and I couldn't be happier with my job.

I have always told women who call my radio show agonizing about their decision and how it might impact their self-worth that the woman is the soul, spirit, and center of a home.

Then came the Alice Walker types; Walker, revered as a trail-blazing feminist and author who touched the lives of a generation of women, proclaimed motherhood as about the worst thing that could happen to a woman. She compared being a mother, raising children, and running a home to slavery—that's right, slavery! Follow that up with Gloria Steinem's declaration that stay-at-home moms were valueless, and what young woman in her right mind would choose to become a valueless slave?

Since that time young women have barely given a thought to this sacrifice of personhood, and have sought independence whatever the cost to their children and marriages—assuming they've even bothered with marriages, when "shack-up" situations give you the freedom to hit the eject button whenever the mood strikes. Obviously, women's independence requires children's independence; hence the drive toward kids being separated from parents and home as early as possible, going into day care or preschool or the care of nannies or babysitters for up to twenty-four hours in a day, regardless of illness and ferocious tears. GPS cell-phone combos now enable busy moms to enjoy the fantasy of being wirelessly connected to kids who are who knows where, and fifty-fifty custody arrangements give moms that career and dating time.

Let's be serious: Who in her right mind would give up all that freedom and opportunity to cook, clean, fold clothes, and keep children busy all day, and then have to cater to the needs of a husband who saunters through that front door at night after having a fun day at work? Yipes! When you put it that way . . .

LIKE MOTHER, LIKE DAUGHTER

People generally plan to have households and relationships that run about the same way as their original family. It therefore shouldn't surprise anyone when the adult daughters of stay-at-home moms (SAHMs) choose to do the same; after all, it is what they are most familiar with, and therefore what they imagine and hope they will get the most family support for. For these women, a childhood with a SAHM gave them a sense of purpose and positive identity with respect to hands-on parenting. They also often describe a sense of obligation and duty as a mother to be their children's primary caregiver, in spite of an all-too-common societal perspective that this amounts to servitude.

Those women whose mothers worked generally also intend to work, because their own moms have given them the idea that being a SAHM is boring and unfulfilling—a curious thing to say to your children about taking care of them, don't you think?

Some women had mothers who offered day care in their own homes so they could stay at home. These women, having seen with their own eyes how their moms spent more time with those children than their own parents did, may have decided that they wanted to be the ones raising their own children.

One woman wrote to me of her very own family experiment. It seems her mother was a SAHM while she was growing up, but then went to school and started to work more and more, so that the writer's younger sisters got less and less of their mom. She described their lives as being "punctuated with shacking up, eating disorders, an abusive husband, divorce, poverty and a child born out of wedlock. I got the best of our mom. Recognizing the difference between our lives, it made me want the best for my future children: a SAHM."

Now, of course I realize that this is an anecdotal situation that cannot be generalized to all family situations, but it does seem logical that hands on, face-to-face interactions during the length of a day between a child and his mother ought to have some kind of profoundly benevolent impact that lasts a lifetime. Or do we really want to believe that human children are no more complex than a goldfish, whose emotional, psychological, and even physical needs might be satisfied with any bowl in any environment as long as there is food to consume? Or is logic not a part of the discussion? Perhaps not.

Unless their mothers ran cathouses or often lay prone on the couch in a drunken stupor, women who had SAHMs describe always feeling safe and cared for, and they want their children to have that same sense of security. I remember feeling the same way; even though my stay-at-home mom lacked the warmth I yearned for, nonetheless having her home made a big emotional difference to me.

Some women hear their own moms' regrets that they didn't stay home, whether for reasons of ego or finances. They hear their moms' lament at not being there for all the important moments that seem so small but are huge when infused with regret and loss: the first cookie, the first boo-boo, the first . . . anything. And it isn't only the "firsts" that make such an emotional impact, especially over the years. It is the ongoing epic of ups and downs, surprises, problems, dramas, curious moments, confused or fearful instances, and so forth, which were handled by someone else who influenced these mothers' children with other than their own heart, soul, psyche, spirit, and knowledge. When the moms express that regret and longing, their adult daughters are understandably impressed with what is indeed a higher purpose, not a cop-out from the feminista movement. Their adult daughters also think about how much they missed having a mommy at home to dote on them, support them, teach them, have fun with them, and just be there. They don't want their kids to miss out on that special feeling.

Following are some of the commentaries I've received that express deep feelings of needing, wanting, or missing a SAHM:

> Dr. Laura, my mother died when I was twelve. I walked to an empty house every day during those precious years. I vowed to myself that I would

always be there for my children as long as [God] allowed me to.

My mom was the mom that would work long hours and missed out on everything I did in school. I realized that I was turning into her, and I remember how I felt when she didn't show up to things I was in and I couldn't do it to my kids anymore.

My mother died when I was twelve, and because my father was often out of town at work I was sent to a series of boarding schools. I was lonely and miserable; all I wanted was to have a normal family life, and I missed my mother terribly. I was exposed to alcohol, drugs, and girls having sex, as they were all searching for the same thing I was: love and security. I knew that when I had children I would always be there for them.

My parents divorced when I was two; my own mother worked two jobs. I never went to day care, but I was constantly bounced around from one family member's house to another, and I remember feeling constant anxiety about it. I wanted nothing more than to stay with my mommy, and it was so

*excruciating to see her drive off to work every day
and every night. I was certain I absolutely would
not have a baby only to leave it day after day.*

*I got pregnant, our baby grew in my body for
nine months, I gave birth, I breast-fed . . . I AM
THE MOMMY!*

TOO MUCH ON THE PLATE

One listener informed me of a new television show on
the ABC network called *Cashmere Mafia*. Evidently,
according to her e-mail, it shows four women in power
suits, sitting at their executive desks, while the voice-
over proclaims that they can have it all, as long as they
have each other.

She continued, "I was given the option of 'having it
all' by society's standards, and I have come to the conclusion that I don't want it all! I just want my son!

"It hit me one day that while I go to work, my house
doesn't get cleaned and supper does not get cooked, so
my husband and son get a very stressed-out wife and
mom when I am at home in the evenings, and that is
not fair to them!"

Well, the obvious answer to this problem is to hire a
housekeeper, a cook, a personal assistant to take care of

errands and calls, a nanny as a surrogate mother, and a surrogate sex partner for the husband, who largely bears the brunt of the exhaustion, resentment, and outright anger of his overworked, frenzied spouse, who oddly comes to see sex as yet another burden rather than the blessed oasis it ought to be.

"My husband and I decided it was time for me to become a SAHM mostly because our family life had become a rat race. To put it simply, it was a frantic rush from the moment I woke up in the morning to try to get everything done at home, and then try to get everything done at work, only to go back home and finish up what I didn't get to in the morning," wrote another woman who had had a prestigious career in law enforcement and wasn't enthusiastic about giving it up. "After all, it was part of my identity!

"My husband and I were basically two ships passing in the night," she said, "and in the months when I worked evenings, I didn't see my kids at all."

The feministas who still wreak havoc on women's minds concerning marriage and maintaining home and family by suggesting they're simply becoming slaves or subordinates ignore at least two important facts. One, many women can and do enjoy creating the nestlike atmosphere of the home and family; and two, a family situation is like a factory: it all works better when there is a division of labor instead of everyone competing to either do or avoid the same task.

Sometimes women experiment with the concept of being a SAHM while bringing their work home with them, only to discover that they still can't "do it all," even in fuzzy slippers; children don't nap on command, nor do their needs for food, nurturance, holding, and playing go on hold until Mom catches up with e-mails. That's typically why the kids or the husband get yelled at, but certainly not the client on the phone!

I realized that most of my income would go to child care plus extra gas, because I would have to travel extra distance for that. I would also have to get up extra early to make all that happen, on top of getting home much later, say 7:00 PM. That would mean I would spend an hour or so a day with my kid—only to put him or her to bed at 8:00 PM? This just didn't sound right. I waited what seemed like my whole life to be a mommy to only get an hour a day?

It generally comes down to exhaustion: tired of being tired and juggling business or work and a family, with the wild scheduling of activities and responsibility that demands, many women reach the conclusion that stay-at-home motherhood is the way to go. As one now-SAHM listener related, "I always noticed a great decrease in the quality of life when Mom was working. She was under considerably more stress and was not as effective as a parent: less warm, more reactive, able to meet fewer needs, less discipline, etc."

While women find the transition from frenetic schedules and work environments to SAHMhood emotionally jarring (this is an issue I will deal with throughout the rest of this book), most women who make the change ultimately find peace and happiness and a profound sense of importance they didn't anticipate.

CAN'T HIRE LOVE?

One of my listeners said it ever so simply: "No other person could raise my newborn with as much love as I could." Truly, you can hire someone to do maintenance (diapers, food, stroller walks, naps, safety issues), but you certainly cannot buy or rent love. And cooing over a closed-circuit TV setup or Internet camera or nanny-cam connection is not the kind of "love" that impacts the child.

So many SAHMs, as well as their adult children, have told me that their homes were the center of the universe for the neighborhood children because there was a mom there for snacks and conversation as well as playtime organization.

I remember, earlier in my career in radio, taking a call one evening from a distraught mother who wanted advice on how to get her two-year-old to call her, not the full-time babysitter, Mommy. My response was, "Gosh, I'm so sorry, but that child is not concerned about the original uterus that enveloped her for nine months; she is only aware of who is always there for her now—and that isn't you."

This woman was one of those single-by-choice women who decided that having the money to pay for home, food, and babysitter was a sufficient qualification for bringing a child into the world and earning the title of Mommy. Obviously, I—and all babies—disagree.

I suggested she stay home all day with the child and then work at night while the child slept.

One listener related to me that her son would always tell her he loved her after she told him she loved him. But it wasn't until she quit work that she noticed he was telling her first. Now she could be there for school functions and extracurricular activities, and to give solace after a bad day or a high five after a particularly good one. All of those interactions fed the "love machine."

Until Hillary Clinton declared that she was not a Tammy Wynette type, baking cookies for the kiddies, the smells, sights, and memories of childhood usually had to do with the lovely and loving things mommies did to make the house a home.

One mother of three children recently called me to complain about her "egocentric" (her word) husband. Evidently he had the temerity to try to assert his opinion in his own home. The woman had moved her mother and father into their home so she could work full-time. The grandparents literally ran the home, taking care of the cleaning and cooking and all child care.

"She is a wonderful mother—the best, the most loving mother," my caller asserted, as though to reassure me that her children were well cared for. And, of course, they were being well taken care of by their doting grandparents.

"The sad thing," I replied, "is that I will never get a call from your children saying any of that about you— they'll be saying it about their grandmother. And your husband doesn't live in his own castle—it is run by your parents. How frustrated is he? And you're here to complain about him?"

I suggested she move her parents out, quit her job, and create those loving memories for her children, her husband, and herself. At first she sputtered, but then she quietly offered, "Thank you, I know what to do."

As one SAHM listener wrote, "Falling in love with my child made me stay at home. Not wanting to give up breastfeeding; basically not wanting to miss a single thing."

It's all about the love.

BEEN THERE—SAW DAY CARE

I have never, and I mean *never*, in thirty-two years of radio, had a nanny, full-time babysitter, or day-care center worker ever tell me that after her job experiences she would ever turn her kids over to nannies, day-care centers, or babysitters! I have had tons of schoolteachers tell me they can tell the difference between kids raised by mommies and those not: "I was a nanny and teacher for many years before we married, and I knew that I did not want anyone else raising our children. I knew from being a nanny that the one who spends the most time with the children truly becomes the momma. I wanted my kids to know beyond a shadow of a doubt that I was their momma."

Another listener wrote, "I decided to be a SAHM because I could not stand the thought of someone else raising my child. I cannot imagine missing all their milestones and not being the person to kiss their boo-boos."

Many women wrote me with horror stories about day care. One woman grew up in a home where her mother did day care. She said that almost all of the kids she watched were moody, mean, or rude, or displayed other such bad behaviors—mostly to get attention. Remember that squeaky wheel?

Another current SAHM wrote,

> I worked in day-care centers between the ages of sixteen and twenty-four. I raised many a child in that context under the guise of the parents sending them to "preschool." "Preschool" was usually open from 6:00 AM to 6:00 PM, and children would spend the majority of that time with me, eating their meals, having their afternoon naps, experiencing daily childhood ups and down, laughing and crying and learning about love and life from me and others like me.
>
> I would often be employed additionally to babysit in these families' homes after hours in the evenings and on weekends—sometimes the entire weekend.
>
> I even worked at a twenty-four-hour day-care center and put kids to bed in a large warehouse-style room on little cots and soothed them in the night when they awoke, feeling all alone in a room full of other children and staff.
>
> Even though I was very late to mature and become a Dr. Laura fan, I had the Dr. Laura voice

in my head all along. At work, it would scream at me, "What are these people doing? Why don't they want to be the ones to read the books, listen to the funny quips from their child's view of the world, and take them to the zoo?"

I made the plan. I knew what spending day after day with kids was all about, and I wasn't going to allow someone else to do the job I feel I was put on the earth to do with my kids. There was no question, really. I can't imagine doing it any other way.

I remember being interviewed by Katie Couric on NBC's *Today Show* about this very issue. She said, in defense of career mothers like herself, that working and doing important things is great role modeling for children, and it also gives them something about their parents to be proud of.

Whew! I came back with, "You don't have kids to have an approving audience. You have kids for their sakes, not your own. Children have very specific emotional and psychological needs, best met by a loving parent, not hired help. I'm a working mom, but my work always came after the needs of our son so that I was always there as the mommy."

I believe a child needs to know that his mother loves him more than she loves a job, career, fame, power, money, prestige, or celebrity. As a psychotherapist who was for many years in practice as a marriage, family, and child therapist in Hollywood, I'm saddened to remember the pain, isolation, and sense of unimportance so many children of the famous struggled with. No, our children are not there to be our cheerleaders; we are here to be theirs.

One mother, now a SAHM, wrote to me and revealed what must have been unbearably painful to admit:

It took three years of being a working mother to convince me to become a SAHM. My first son was in day care for six weeks, and people kept telling me he'd be just fine and I should stop worrying because he was in the best day care in town.

But I missed him terribly. We arranged our schedule so that my husband dropped our son off as late as possible in the morning while I went to work very early so I could pick him up as early as possible. That meant I never saw him in the morning before I left.

I am ashamed to admit that once, when he was so very young, I went to pick him up and didn't recognize him. I had not seen him that morning, it was early enough in his life that I was working on very little sleep, I was totally stressed out . . . but none of that negates the fact that for a moment, I didn't recognize my own baby.

It was only for a moment, till I looked into those eyes and really saw him. But that's just it—I was always so busy and so harried that I never really saw him. I never really saw my husband either, or my house.

Dr. Laura, the first time I heard you call day care a warehouse (or day orphanage) I was offended. But I kept listening to you, and you got into my head.

Within six months they worked it out, and she was home with her child, having those precious millions of one-on-one quality moments.

Another mother related that her mom worked full-time and that she was a day-care kid. "I not only hated it, but I had a few traumatic experiences at the day-care center. I would never put my own children at risk like that."

I'm sure there are many pleasant and safe day cares, with lovely people servicing the children. But day care is an enclosed and limited experience where children have to fight to claim attention, or withdraw from the pain of it all. With you, a SAHM, they get to chase butterflies, help with meals, go on errands and adventures, get explanations and inspiration, nap and open their eyes and see their mommy's smiling, loving face, play with food, and on and on and on. Most importantly, they're in an environment that is familiar, filled with the sounds, sights, and smells of family, and with a person who makes them the center of the universe at a developmental period when they need that security.

No matter how technologically and aesthetically spectacular a day care is, no matter how prestigious and expensive or cheap and available, there is no way on God's earth it can even compare to, much less surpass, the loving presence of a mother.

DR. LAURA MADE ME DO IT

One of my listeners wrote,

> *Seriously, it was your nagging, Dr. Laura. I had my first child in 1995 and had been listening to you for a few years, but it didn't come through to me until after I gave birth to that child.*
>
> *I always thought when I had children I would work; my mother was in the military, and I just thought you put children in child care. When my husband and I decided we wanted to have children, I was a short-time listener to Dr. Laura and just*

had a lightbulb moment when I heard her talk about being "her kid's mom." Something just changed, and I knew that no one else would raise my children but my husband and me. About a year later I became pregnant. Once I had my first daughter, I never went back to work—that was about eight years ago.

I'm proud to say that I've gotten innumerable letters from listeners blaming becoming a SAHM on me—and being quite grateful for it.

A recent caller, who was having a "transition" problem (I'll be dealing with that issue later in this book), told me that her kids were happier and that her husband said that the stress level in the home had dropped dramatically and that it was lovely to see her there for the children, and for her to have so much left for him. He also expressed pride at having to work harder to take care of the family.

As I mentioned earlier, child care is not just a maintenance program for both ends of the child. What do you want your children to think is right and wrong? How do you want them to see life and death? What do you hope they'll learn and practice about compassion? How do you want them to approach a relationship with God? Who do you want to teach them about bullies, friends, pets, school, relatives, hurts, fears, or disappointments? What habits do you want them to develop? How can you imagine being the one your children will go to when there are problems or trouble if you are not the primary caregiver . . . the mommy?

There is no such thing as quality time as an entity separate from quantity time. You can never know when a moment of angst or curiosity will hit your child, and you have to be responsive to that moment or feeling in your special way. Quality moments occur only when there is quantity time for them to spontaneously occur.

As I told one mother, "Sure, you can pump your breast milk into a bottle for anyone to administer to your child. But what does it mean to you and your child when he is taking nourishment directly from your breast as you hold him in your arms and look lovingly into each other's eyes?" She cried.

Fortunately, I'm not the only influential woman out there (though we are few and far between) to remind women of their blessed importance in a child's development and family life. One listener wrote that she had always planned to be a career mom. That is, until she took a course in developmental psychology from a wonderful and wise woman who had raised her own children *and then* went to college and graduate school and began teaching.

The listener wrote, "She took every opportunity during class to say to her students how very important it was for a mom to stay at home with her children during their early years. And she emphasized as well how those children needed a mom when they came home from school too; and that those needs change as the children grow, but don't diminish in importance, whether for an infant, toddler, preschooler, grade-schooler, or high-schooler."

It is not accidental that this course was in a private religious college. The secular collegiate environment is fraught with antimom/antiwife women's studies feministas who would never suggest that children need their own mommies. You know, I not so secretly doubt that any of those feministas would have chosen day care or nannies rather than a loving mother for themselves.

Summary Thought

I have two kids, ages eight and six. I've been a SAHM for about eighteen months, after being a career mom who worked forty hours a week on flextime. I decided to become a SAHM because I was tired of juggling my full-time job and caring for my family. I was doing neither to the best of my ability, and feeling pulled between them both at all times.

My children were getting involved in more activities, and I was finding myself wishing I could spend more time with them. As the kids grew, I found I liked them more and more, as their personalities developed and they turned into "real" people.

The older they got, the more I felt like they needed more grown-up guidance, and I wanted to be the person to provide that.

2

THE STAY-AT-HOME MOM'S INNER STRUGGLES

Deciding to be a SAHM is just the beginning of a sometimes difficult journey. More than one new SAHM has called me on my radio program to say, "I'm embarrassed to tell you this, but I'm not happy." These women believe it is the best thing for their children and their family life, but are overwhelmed, confused, lost, and often downright miserable.

One listener mom recently wrote,

I am a stay-at-home mom to three children, 4½, 2½, and 1. Long story short . . . I am crazed, fried, and overwhelmed much of the time. My husband and I admittedly have chosen a parenting path that is not easy: our kids don't watch TV, so I don't have an automatic babysitter when I feel "incon-

venienced" by their energy and "childishness." We have chosen to homeschool, so I don't see a "break" in my future. The baby wants to nurse, while my daughter is spinning in circles begging to go outside, and my son is crying because he doesn't understand that his cookie is "broken" because he took a bite out of it.

I have been prone to complaining, dreading the day, always looking for the time when they will be asleep, feeling like I don't like my job.

The stresses and strains of being an at-home mom are real and difficult. In fact, many women transitioning into SAHMhood feel like everything comfortable and familiar in their lives has been yanked out from under them.

Another newbie SAHM wrote that I was the only one in the world who supported her and helped her believe she was doing the right thing. At first, she felt like less of a person, leaving her professional life to be "just" a mom. After listening to me day after day reinforce the importance of a mom to a child, she realized that in fact she had been brainwashed to believe that motherhood was beneath the dignity of an intelligent, independent woman. She would watch people's eyes glaze over when she told them she was a SAHM, and she felt like she had to rush in with a "but, before I left I was . . . ," as if to prove her intelligence to them.

She also expressed a fear that she seemed to share with a lot of SAHMs: not believing she could be a good enough mother. She felt that by hiring a nanny or babysitter, or putting the child in day care, she could avoid any of the mistakes she might make.

As for the first mom mentioned above, the one "feeling like I don't like my job," there is a reassuring happy ending.

> *Tonight, as I lay next to my four-year-old daughter, rubbing her back, singing a song, helping her fall asleep, she looked at me with tears in her eyes, grabbed my face with both hands, and said with such love and conviction, "YOU are my lullaby, Mommy."*
>
> *I cried right then and there, and the tears continued to flow as she slept in my arms. No, I don't get to have a latte at ten, go to lunch with co-workers, and go out for drinks after work. I am not being overseen by someone who gives me performance-based raises and praise. Instead, I am in the most beautiful and profound position I could ever hold. I am my daughter's lullaby; the mundane parts of my job are elevated to the loftiest*

heights when I am held in HER esteem—not MY self-esteem. I will know that it was ME who taught her to love truly, and give her husband and children a legacy of devotion and commitment.

I'M JUST NO LONGER IMPORTANT

Many of the women who have called my radio program needing that last bit of moral support before they submit their two weeks' notice report that it is one of the hardest things they've ever had to do. Why? Without having experienced children calling you "their lullaby," you'll probably feel like you're going from a job or career in which you get daily ego boosts to a situation where there is no compensation or psychological or emotional reward.

It's not only that your work defined who you were; many of you love your jobs and careers because of the stimulation and camaraderie, because of the goals you accomplish, and because of the financial remuneration that leads you to feel like you are really and truly contributing to the family.

"Motherhood and apple pie" once stood for the ultimate gift of being an American in a great country. Now, women who choose motherhood feel they risk being viewed as someone who will not work, is lazy, or just can't cut it in the real world. Many of you SAHMs are suffering from feeling undervalued as a person because you chose to stay at home—as though you are no longer a productive person in society and in your home.

I get phone calls to my radio show from women whose moms are actually supporting the notion that they are wasting their lives and intelligence by raising their children. More often than not, these "grandmothers," as I tell the callers, "are acting out their guilt for not raising you. If they can get you to do what they did, then they feel less guilt." It is tough, though, when your own mother undermines your commitment to being there with your children for each of their "firsts"—whether roll-over, step, or word—and teaching them the way of the world through your values.

Yet one of the major aspects of not being a SAHM is that you are visible in the world—seen coming and going and being responsible for things. For some women, a sense of invisibility strikes once they are at home with children; all of a SAHM's "work responsibilities" are within the walls of her residence, where she is generally alone. Since no goal is ever really accomplished for good—no kitchen cupboard stays stocked, no diaper stays unfilled, and no bathroom stays clean—her repetitive efforts can feel thankless and unnoticed. This is where a good husband comes in—one who expresses appreciation and gratitude for the woman who is raising his children and creating a lovely, peaceful, happy home for all of them.

I have had to remind more than one tired, cranky husband who comes home to see a less than totally put-together house, or one in some child-friendly disarray, to remember that while he got coffee breaks, alone time in his commute, chat time with colleagues, and accolades for completed jobs, his wife was putting every minute of the day into the sanctuary he just came home to, and he owes her much respect, no matter how frustrated or frazzled he is. (Actually, this concept does go two ways—thought I'd just throw that in.)

There are some concrete goals a SAHM can have, ranging from taking care of the finances and creating the budget to learning home repair or designing the garden. And once the children are in school, those hours are yours!

Ultimately, the value of a SAHM can indeed be measured, both in the home and in society. As one SAHM wrote to me:

> Over the years I have seen the degeneration of society as women go to work and leave their children alone or with others. For the most part, mothers instill the moral values in children. Since

prayer and godly values have been taken out of the schools, the children have become increasingly sullen, rebellious, unthankful, uncaring, selfish, and inconsiderate. I want to do my part to help my children become positive contributors to society and embrace godly principles and actions. I feel this can be accomplished best by staying with them and creating a home environment where they can be safe and loved and will thrive.

WHO'S IN CONTROL?

The older you are when you decide to marry and have children, the more ingrained you are with your own habits, and the more control you've been used to having over your own life. When I had our son, over two decades ago when I was thirty-eight, I was a professional woman with five or six jobs! It was remarkable to me that something that barely weighed anything, couldn't roll over on its own, couldn't feed itself, and couldn't talk to me literally ruled me, my husband, our time, and our home. I would start working on something, and that's just when our son would wake up from his two-minute nap! There were days I didn't shower until my husband came home.

One now-SAHM wrote,

I didn't meet my husband until my mid-thirties, so when I gave birth to my son, I had been settled in my career-oriented life, and when the time came, it was very difficult to give that up. It was easy to make the decision in theory, but in practice it meant giving up what I considered to be my identity and my reason for living: work. I thought that teaching gave my life meaning (and it did), and it felt somewhat empty to be home alone with a screaming newborn.

I am somewhat of a control freak, and a child is not something you can control in any way. It felt very "messy" being a mother at home, not getting to eat or sleep or even shower when I wanted to.

This SAHM made the transition by realizing that her prior career as a teacher is something she's doing every day with a brand-new person—her child—as well as with the children who come to play. Managing all the needs and feelings of her family, taking care of all the basics, and figuring out clever ways to manage the complex entity that is a "home and family" is challenge enough, she found.

Another SAHM wrote, "My difficulty was in not being intellectually stimulated with a one-year-old. But I've overcome that by being on the board of directors for a small company, where I call in during board meetings—sometimes with a baby attached to me . . . feeding."

Nonetheless, that feeling of being "trapped" is probably a typical reaction to the reality of the relentless needs of an infant or small child. The diminished income puts serious limitations on activities (I remember a friend gifting me $50 so that our son could play T-ball) and often makes a second car an unaffordable luxury (I developed fabulous leg muscles bike-riding our son everywhere until we were able to afford a second car). Add to that the attacks of boredom (which I made up for by taking up machine knitting); the sense of loneliness, as you may not have much SAHM company while you watch other moms seep back into work; the frustration of watching all your resources (time, energy, attention, money) go into parenting and missing the freedom of a little shopping for fun things you really don't need; and the reality that a nine-to-five job meant you were actually off at five—but now your work is twenty-four/seven!

Take-charge women who choose to be SAHMs sometimes have a real problem with the fact that you can never really get anything under control; children are by nature unpredictable and resistant to organization, as is the plumbing and the temperature of the oven. To paraphrase an e-mail from one SAHM, you'll have to relax your exacting standards, surrender the dream of a perfectly organized home with every-thing in its place, and give up your ideal of perpetually well-behaved children. You have to either assume that attitude and perspective—or go nuts!

For the first year or two of our son's life, I consid-ered the house a giant toy box with food and just didn't worry about how it looked. I concerned myself only with clean—and trust me, I love things in order, so that was tough for me too!

Stepping way outside your comfort zone is a scary, but finally terrific, experience. Many of you SAHMs have found ways to be of service that take you outside your daily home experiences without interfering or un-dermining them because you and your children are "in it together." For example, get involved in play groups, exercise, volunteering for children's programs, church and civic activities that are family oriented, and so forth. I took our son everywhere with me, and frankly, that is one of the best parts of being a SAHM: when you have your child with you and you're both involved in some outside activities, you not only have more bond-ing time, but your child is exposed to a wide range of real-world activities and people—an exposure he obvi-ously cannot get in a day-care center.

WHY THE GUILT?

You know, I've read zillions of women's magazine articles telling women they shouldn't feel guilty for putting their kids in day care. I can hardly remember seeing one such magazine have a cover story on not feeling guilty for being a SAHM instead of a wage earner.

It makes me both sad and mad that so many women who are thinking about becoming SAHMs have to deal with a sense of guilt that their husbands are burdened financially because they have to provide for the family alone.

"It was tough," wrote a SAHM, "the first time I didn't get a paycheck. I felt some pressure to perform if I wasn't contributing any $$." Isn't it sad that importance in the world and in the family has become so tightly associated with money? Isn't it sad that a difference in roles (homemaker versus financial provider) has come to mean a difference in value as a human being? Isn't it sad that so many children have been dying in day-care centers and overheated cars because the value of an adult in our society has been so disassociated from parenting and associated with two busy, busy careers? Isn't it sad that so many young folk are "shacking up" instead of marrying because they didn't have family role models, and *The Waltons* sadly is no longer on television?

As I have said not enough times on my radio program, there was a time when a young man would not even think of dating, much less marrying, until he was financially stable enough to support a family. This seemingly obvious concept is not for the purpose of oppressing women; it is for the express purpose of revering women and the children forthcoming.

Nonetheless, current feminista mentality is that men are largely irrelevant as husbands and fathers, and a woman's place is anywhere besides the home; what happened to the concept of choices?

Many women call me, complaining that the guy they're dating or have already married does not wish to be the sole supporter, or to give up the perks of that second salary. I tell the unmarried ladies to dump the guy and be patient enough to wait to marry a man who shares their values and view of family and parenthood. I tell the married ladies to sit down on their own, make up a budget, and present it to their husbands, avoiding any argument by saying only, "Honey, I know this is a challenge, but I know you're man enough to do this for us. I know you can take care of us while I raise our children and make this house the warmest home of any man you know."

Forget "if" and get right to the "how"—and do it. Trust that you will make it work out. Once you're committed to the goal, you stop wasting energy on debate and worry, and instead stay focused on making it happen. When you do that, the sacrifices and the transition issues will seem huge—but in retrospect, they'll be experiences to smile over and hold hands and reminisce about.

Those guys who take no pride in providing for and protecting their families as men—not unisex couples—are generally the offspring of feminista types and/or broken homes. Once their women support their masculine sense of taking care of family, these men generally profess to feel better about themselves and their lives. The ones who don't, sadly, are just going to spend more time as boys or males, rather than men.

So women, choose wisely. If you're already in the position of having a boy/male husband, work very hard to boost his masculine sense, but don't wait for that to happen before you take care of your children. Just make the decision—make the plan, make the best of it, make him feel like a hero for going along with you. And be patient—sometimes it takes a bit of time for him to reclaim the masculinity that our society has robbed him of. Don't have fights over it; he's really saying "no way" because he's scared—unless, of course, you married a real jerk. Assuming the latter is not the case, just keep reinforcing how you just know "your man" will make it happen.

Remind him that the flip side of this is an issue for you. For the first time since your childhood, you are going to depend on somebody else for your well-being. And tell him you can do that only because you know he's man enough for the job, and you can trust and depend on him.

Arguing will get you nowhere, and you will probably both say horrible things to each other—including some things that might never be forgotten. Instead . . . pump him up!

Some women thinking of becoming SAHMs but who have resistant husbands worry about a divorce. And you know what? Sometimes that does happen. One SAHM wrote that her husband basically refused to take on the "burden" of being the wage earner. After they divorced, she took care of the children on her own all day, and then got someone to be there when she worked in the evening. After a while, her ex admitted that he was incredibly impressed with her commitment and realized that having a mother there was everything to these children. I'm hoping they got back together.

But most of the time a divorce—even after the threat—doesn't happen. Why? Because very few husbands and fathers want to lose their families. I've asked these male callers, "Do you really want to lose those everyday hugs and smiles from your little ones? Do you really want to be visiting your children instead of raising them? Do you really believe your wife is being selfish or demanding by wanting to touch your children's faces when they're sad or laugh with them when they're glad? Do you really want to give up that warm, loving body by your side each night? Do you really want to lose all of that, instead of losing some toys and income? Do you really?"

I haven't had a guy say, "Yes," not even once. I've heard guys cry, though.

I AM WOMAN—WATCH ME PURR

I know many of you contemplating becoming SAHMs are struggling with letting go of your pride, your income, and your professional status to let your husband be the "man" in your home. While he is being the "man," you are being the "woman." As time goes on, you will experience the wondrous feeling of being the center of your family, the one everyone turns to. Have you noticed that when the mother passes away, families often drift apart? It is so sad to see that—but it highlights my point that the matriarch is the glue of family and community.

When I published *The Proper Care and Feeding of Husbands*, I was really trying to resurrect that

months in utero). I thought those years at home were very difficult (especially when they cry before they've learned to speak, and you don't know what the heck is going on!)—but those are the years that deepened my understanding and compassion, demanded I learn more patience, made me feel important whenever I heard that little voice call, "Mama," and enriched my life more than I could ever imagine.

So think about it less as "Is that all there is?" and more as "I can't believe how much I have."

AND THEN WHAT?

How many times have you watched some television chick flick where the female protagonist was complaining about just being a wife and a "mother," and how she didn't know who she was? What was that supposed to mean? Was it to suggest that self-fulfillment is best met without obligations to anyone else? Was it to suggest that a new man, a job, a new life, would better define her? As a what? Having a man adore and take care of you makes you a woman. Having a child adore and learn from you makes you a woman. Is a woman better defined by sexual adventures and no responsibilities?

I don't think so.

It is true that you can place yourself in a rut. Some difficult times (like when children are teething or the bills are tough to keep up with) have to be endured. But even in those difficult times, playing music at dinner, taking walks in the evening, reading, taking time to paint or fool around on the piano, exercising, playing board games, and on and on all bring novelty into what has to be a reasonably respected schedule of responsibilities.

So don't whine—create!

As one SAHM put it,

> For a short while I wanted to go to work to be "independent" and make myself happy because I felt like I was "just a mom." I wasn't satisfied until one day I woke up and realized how blessed I really was to have this time with my children and to be able to stay home with them and have that "pot of beans" ready for them when they get home.
>
> Now I stay home because I know it is the best thing for them to have Mommy there taking care of them, helping them with homework and other things, and taking care of their home sweet home.

The time spent on family is not a sacrifice. You are living a life with choices; when you make the right ones, you have a good life. You are defined by the choices in your life—and that is a good thing!

Summary Thought

I decided to be a SAHM because my children's spirits, well-being, character, and future were extremely important to my husband and me. I couldn't stand the thought of someone else seeing them take that first step, hearing their first words, and so forth. It was tough, but my husband—their father—and I made a commitment almost twenty years ago to stay together and put them first in every aspect of our lives and marriage.

I am proud of us because I know we have done that. The difficulty we had to face inside ourselves was to not think of ourselves first. My husband has worked hard for two decades, always providing for us physically, mentally, and financially. He has always put us first and taken care of our needs.

My husband and I knew that our jobs as a family were not just to call ourselves parents but to BE mother and father, husband and wife. We knew that those titles are earned, not just a right. What my children grow up with they will follow and execute; that is and was very important to us.

These words came from a SAHM who has been there and done that.

3

THE NAYSAYERS

If there is one group in America that dearly needs cheerleaders, it is SAHMs. Although I didn't watch the program, I received scores of shocked and angry letters about how one television program dealt with the issue of SAHMs. Evidently, the most successful afternoon "women's" television show recently had as a guest the most successful female television financial adviser, and the result was a virtual hurricane of mail I received, expressing rage at the complete dismissal of even the possibility of becoming a SAHM as an intelligent choice.

Apparently the discussion was about family budgeting, and the situation in question was a mom and dad and children with a combined income of $6,600 per month. This family owned two homes and two expensive cars. According to one SAHM listener,

You can imagine my surprise to learn that "mom" only earned $2,000 per month, and their day-care cost exceeded $1,800 per month. I assumed that [the woman adviser] was going to recommend that "mom" stay home. Instead, to my surprise, the "feminazi" ordered the family to uproot their children and sell everything, move to an apartment, and continue to work—and that "mom" might want to consider a second job!

As I lifted myself up from the floor from this ridiculous advice given to these people, I proceeded to throw myself from the chair again when [the adviser] advised an overspending mother of six children—yes, six!—to seek employment out of the home, as she needed to contribute income to the household. At that point I began to ponder what exactly it was that [the adviser] was an "expert" at—obviously, it was just the money.

Then there is the TLC cable channel's so-called reality show *The Secret Life of a Soccer Mom*. Simply put, it is geared toward seducing SAHMs away from their children and families. Here's the description from the TLC Web site:

TLC picked up The Secret Life of a Soccer Mom, *a one-hour reality show that takes ordinary*

*stay-at-home mothers and shows them what their
lives could have been like had they pursued their
careers instead of taking care of the family.*

*Moms who have always wanted to be chefs, po-
lice officers, fashion designers, and others will be
able to pursue their careers for one week. At the
end of the week, the mom can either choose to live
the dual life of raising a family and having a career
or go back to being a stay-at-home parent.*

*Almost every woman experiences the pull be-
tween becoming a full-time mom or juggling both
family and work. This show will give us the chance
to learn what sacrifices and rewards there are in
making this challenging and unique decision.*

*TLC senior vice president of programming,
Brant Pinvidic, said in a statement, "Each episode
ends up being a remarkable voyage as we see them
accomplish goals they never thought possible and
then make the decision about which path they
should pursue."*

There's so much wrong with this, I don't know
where to start:

- "Ordinary" stay-at-home mothers? What is ordinary about "the hand that rocks the cradle

rules the world"? The individual who nurtures, teaches, and loves a developing human being is worthy of the highest esteem and is hardly "ordinary."

You either choose to have a career, or you choose to stay home to raise your children. There's no duality there. Perhaps this is best answered with an e-mail I got from one SAHM, entitled "Even my 5-year-old gets it!":

As I am cleaning the kitchen, we are listening to you on the computer, Dr. Laura, and my son was working on an art project. I had no idea he was even listening to what you were saying. There was a woman on the radio with two marriages and three children, and she wanted to go to school for Criminal Justice. You were telling her that she needs to be at home with her children—not getting a degree when she is needed by them. You explained that if you work, you come home too tired to fool with your kids, make a home-cooked dinner, or have sex with your husband.

My son said, "Mom, she's right." I say, "Who, honey?" He said, "That girl on the radio. She said if you work, that when you come home you are too tired to play with your kids. Mom, she's right and the other woman is wrong!"

From the mouths of babes!

- *"Sacrifices and rewards"?* I don't think I need to present any statistics and studies to make the point that when a woman who is a mother and a wife leads a "dual life," the sacrifices are made not only by her—in the form of stress, missing the children, a more chaotic home life, a strained marriage—but also by her children and husband, who become neglected (unless you believe that a mother's love and attention are no different from those of hired help).

- "Make a decision about which path they should pursue"? What, they haven't made the decision already? Of course they have; that's why they are SAHMs. A program like this makes women doubt themselves; clearly, TLC is suggesting that they need to be "rescued" from the wrong decision.

I haven't noticed TLC developing a program that takes career women and brings them home to make a decision about which path they should pursue. Have you?

HIP, HIP, HOORAY FOR SAHMS!

Another future SAHM wrote,

> *Thanks for making me be such a good cheerleader to stay-at-home moms and hard-working dads. I'm single, never married, no kids.*
>
> *A SAHM came into my office to pick up a package I was holding for her and her husband. Highly educated and used to a high-powered job, she said that she felt terrible about not working and about being a SAHM because of all the criticism she gets from other women.*
>
> *I told her that she was doing the hardest, most rewarding job in the world, and that her critics were wrong. I reminded her that her husband and kids needed her; what she did for the family meant the world to them, to make great meals for everybody to enjoy and to always be her husband's girlfriend!*
>
> *She left our office smiling, validated, valued, and respected for what she does for her family! Thank you for dismantling the feminist rhetoric (I was formerly one of those bitter, hateful women) and helping me heal the hurts the feminist movement is still inflicting on so many.*

SAHMs are not SAHMs because they're lucky, stupid, lazy, weak, scared, useless, spoiled, frightened, or any other condescending description. SAHMs are SAHMs because they realize the blessing of the opportunity to make a profound difference in their own lives, their families, their community, and ultimately the world as they coordinate the lives of their family members so that no one feels neglected, unimportant, or unloved because of the limited commitment of their parents.

I love reading about the small but growing number of women who are brazenly tooting their own horns in celebration of their commitment to family. One wrote,

> *What irritates me the most is when people ask what I do for a living, and when I say "stay-at-home mom," they dismiss me. DON'T DISMISS ME! What I do is more important than any amount of lawyering or fashion designing or managing that you will EVER do. I may not be getting paid for it in salary, but the giggles, hugs, and "I love you's" that I get on a daily basis are worth more than anything you could imagine. What I do matters. Don't you DARE make me feel otherwise.*

And the super kudos should come from husbands:

When I married the beautiful woman I call my wife, she told me that when we had kids, she was going to stay at home and care for them. I was more liberally minded (so I thought) and didn't believe such a sacrifice was needed, especially as it would cut the family income substantially. Well, it would be nine years until we finally did have a little one, and he is only just a year now, with NO chance of his mom going back to work and abandoning him. My mind was changed by that time, and I realized that my wife had the right idea to begin with—and frankly, wasn't ever really giving me the option.

I am grateful for marrying a SAHM, and though I denied it at the time, I always knew it was the RIGHT decision.

OTHER PEOPLE'S DUMB COMMENTS

I got a huge giggle from one SAHM who wrote me about what she calls her "ex"-aunt. This aunt, the mother of two, was recently divorced from the writer's uncle. While they were out to lunch together, with my writer containing her annoyance at her aunt breaking up her marriage, the aunt said, "I don't know how you quit your job as a teacher to stay at home with your kids.

Don't they drive you crazy? How can you just give up your life like that and waste your college degree?"

Well, you can believe that "dumb comment" was not well received. Our SAHM told me that having listened to my radio program for so long had given her the moxie and words with which to respond: "I haven't given up my life . . . this is my life! My kids are my life, as is my husband. I would not trade it for anything in the world!"

This SAHM was, just three years ago, a career-driven "make as much money as possible" woman, who, after her husband's urging and my nagging on the radio, made the decision to be at home with their two children.

Her last statement: "Maybe if my ex-aunt had spent more time working on her relationship with her husband and taking care of the kids, instead of putting them in day care, she might still be married."

I don't take that as a "snotty" comment, because there is truth to the observation that each of us has just so much energy and time in a day, and our obligations have to be triaged; unfortunately, family issues usually come way after work obligations. When the pressures of work overwhelm a human being, any needs from family become an unbearable burden, and that's precisely when resentments and tempers are elevated.

Home is no longer seen as a sanctuary, an oasis, but as yet another place with demands.

Sadly, this may indeed end up in divorce, as the overwhelmed woman feels her life would be better with the romantic dude met on the Internet or the hiring of a divorce attorney.

A SAHM wrote me that a couple of her coworkers who have children did say to her that they could not stay home with their children: one because she did not want to give up the lifestyle that she can have because she makes good money; the other because she doesn't have the patience—it would drive her crazy to stay home with the kids. This latter coworker moved her mother-in-law into the home to become the surrogate mother.

All I could think of when I read that was, I hope the children never hear her saying that. Can you imagine the pain they'd feel, knowing they were either a burden to their mom's sanity or an impediment to financial gain? Talk about having self-esteem issues!

If this is thrust in your face, gently say, "You're right. Giving up the income, ego, and freedom are very big deals. Giving up the gooey kisses, sticky hand hugs, and those moments when their eyes light up as they discover something . . . well, those are big deals too, and I'm sorry you're missing them." Sympathy is a better argument than criticism.

CONVINCING THE HUSBAND

Men are practical creatures and have been as misled as women to believe that the most important things in life are . . . well . . . things—and things require money. Both husband and wife working, even with children, means more money, which buys more things. It is not unusual for today's "male" to not welcome the idea of his wife's becoming a SAHM, as then he would have to give up things.

While I already presented this subject in chapter 2, it is worthwhile to repeat and amplify some of the concepts. Men are generally not won over by emotion; they are won over by facts. So, give 'em facts. The first is that you are going to quit your job. However, presenting it just like that is like throwing oil on a fire. If you say something like, "I've decided that our lives—your life—will be improved if I stay home because you'd have a happier, more relaxed (and therefore sexier-feeling) wife, the children would be calmer with a consistent caretaker, the home will be more organized and snuggly, and you will be a more content man." This is all something a husband can easily wrap his mind around and come out on the positive side.

Second, crunch the numbers. When he realizes how much money is spent on your commute to work, the clothes and gadgets you need for working, paying the housekeeper and landscaper to take care of the house you don't have that much time to enjoy, and day care, it'll seem like a financial wash.

Third, paint the picture. Start describing life as it is now and talk about your mutual dreams since childhood with respect to what home and family would be. Explore whether or not how things are going mirrors those dreams. Get behind him and rub his shoulders . . . and tell him home will feel just like that.

Fourth, show him respect. Whether or not women wish to admit it, we respect a man more when we can depend on him, count on him, lean on him, trust him to take care of us. Let your husband know that although it might be a bit of a difficult time, you positively, absolutely believe that he is "the man" and will be able to make this happen.

Finally, tell him that "living to work" is not as desirable as "working to live."

One SAHM informed me that her husband had very little empathy for the struggles she faced as a SAHM until he left their restaurant business to help with their third child. Now he is very empathetic and agrees that it is the hardest job on the planet. I think the idea some women have had, of making their husbands take care of everything for one week while they disappear to their mom's house, would be a good cure for the dubious dad.

DAY CARE IS BETTER THAN MOMMA
CARE . . . REALLY?

I just love hearing the argument that day care is good for children because they get to become independent from parents (at six months?) and socialize (at one year?) in ways they can't with a momma. At one time, day care was seen as a temporary measure—sad, but sometimes necessary—meant to rescue parents in dire straits. Now, however, some are actually touting day care as superior to care by a mother. If your mother is an unconscious druggie or drunk, running a bordello from her home, immaturely neglectful, or so mentally incompetent as to be nonfunctional, I guess that statement would be true. However, that is the rare exception and not the rule.

One SAHM wrote, "Most of our friends are dual-income families who put their kids in day care at a very young age. It has been hard to stay comfortable being friends with them due to this huge difference in philosophies. Many, many times they have tried to convince me that I am doing my son a DISSERVICE staying home with him; that I am going to stunt his development because he's not around other kids all day; that he won't be ready for school; and that it's bad for my mental health (which actually is sometimes true . . . but the struggle is worth it)."

I don't for one moment believe that these folks believe that it is better for an infant or a toddler to be in day care than to be home with Mom. I do believe that these folks feel guilty for not wanting to be at home, so they devise a new reality to compensate for their uncomfortable feelings: day care is superior to themselves. And when we want to feel better about ourselves, we try to recruit others to join us, the same way we feel that strawberry cheesecake has less calories if we both have a piece. Nonetheless, I don't think many of us would actually choose other than mothering for ourselves, were we to be recycled and have a choice.

One SAHM wrote to me that her college friends gave her a hard time as they went off to business or law school. Ironically, many of them eventually became SAHMs too—a growing trend, as more and more professional women discover that in spite of all their successes, they feel—as I did—that something is missing from their lives. They just don't feel that satisfied with a life that makes them a visitor in their own home and with their children. She told me that as twenty-somethings, her kids often tell them how glad they were it was *their* mom driving to games or volunteering—even during high school.

> *We all believe my "momness" was a major fac-tor in their becoming confident, kind, responsible, productive young adults. Perfect kids? NO. Won-derful, good, interesting people? YES.*
>
> *Once they came home from Youth Group at church to tell us they were the only ones who didn't have a topic for a discussion of "how to deal with our parent problems." We were surprised at first, but then we realized we have never seen them as problems—challenges, maybe. Now they return the respect.*

I am just not sure that parents can get that same response from children spending their time with sur-rogate caretakers. Seems to me, the caretakers would get the response; but, I could be wrong—right?

YOU'RE JUST WASTED!

Why is it that so many critics of SAHMs get on a tear about women wasting their lives? Since when is being the center of the family universe a waste? Furthermore, one's talents show themselves every day. If you're good at math, you do the finances. If you're good at music, you can expose the family to great music and teach your children—and so forth.

As one SAHM wrote,

> *I heard one of your callers say her boss felt that furthering her education would be a waste once she had children and became a SAHM. That's what I thought when I left my career as an ICU nurse, something I spent years accomplishing and something I loved.*
>
> *I quit to stay home with drooling, pooping babies! At first I thought, "What a waste of my education!" Then I got creative. I started homeschooling them both when they were in the third grade. They're now two wonderful high-school students that have the greatest characters you could ever ask for. They are grounded, well adjusted, intelligent, and wonderful people to be around.*
>
> *Me? My education? I now teach high-school biology, marine biology, and chemistry to other homeschooled students. I used to think nursing was my greatest gift, but I discovered another one: teaching what I love—and I'm the happiest, proudest mom ever.*

One of the more obnoxious statements I sometimes hear about the lifestyle of a SAHM is this notion of fulfillment. Since the 1960s, there has been a shift in values from obligation to fulfillment. An activity has to give pleasure, or it is without true value. If the activity does not make you feel good or feel better about yourself, then its usefulness to your life is questionable.

This is a sad turn of events for the soul of a human being. While sucking on a sweet lollipop gives ongoing pleasure, getting to have one whenever you want doesn't seem like the kind of life experience that actually makes life worth living.

I know that when I get into that darker place and read one of my listener e-mails, grateful for my words, which inspired them to be and do more, I feel fulfilled. When my son called one time from his army base just to tell me that he appreciated my always being there for him when he needed me, I felt fulfilled. However, the pain and aggravation that go along with a radio career and parenting don't feel fulfilling at all. So, that means that tilling the soil, planting the seeds, watering and fertilizing, protecting from the elements, aren't worthwhile activities because in and of themselves, they are not fulfilling? How, then, do you ever get a harvest?

Life is just not always fulfilling. Callers who have to care for the elderly in their families when they already have their own marriages, children, and mortgages to deal with are not necessarily feeling very fulfilled by changing adult diapers and listening to the same stories time and time again. Yet it is in these efforts that we perfect the world.

A sense of fulfillment needs to see forward, and not just at the moment you're cleaning up after a toilet overflow.

One of my favorite stories about SAHM criticism came from a woman who had been a police officer. When she went in to human resources to turn in her equipment and badge, the female superior told her that she was making a big mistake giving up all she had worked so hard for. She tried to explain to the superior that she was doing what she believed to be the right thing for the baby, but that wasn't received with much enthusiasm.

Then, just to change the subject, our SAHM asked her superior about herself and her family. The superior said that she was busy, and that the boys were okay; one was in school, another had a broken arm, and the third was home sick with a 103-degree temperature, being cared for by her soon-to-be-ex-husband.

"At that moment," she wrote, "I thought I had just received the biggest neon sign from God that I was doing the right thing. I walked away from that appointment confident in my decision. Though I was still sad from the loss of my 'identity,' it became clearer to me that my new identity as a mom was far more rewarding and immediately necessary."

A lot of folks critical about SAHMs suggest that working moms are happier. One SAHM related such a story about a working mom:

> *She has children but was unable to stay at home because she had to be the breadwinner. Her rationale to defend working moms as happier: "Yeah, we get to go out to lunch with our friends, we don't have to stay home all day, we get out more, we have our career," etc.*
>
> *I did not want to rub in her face that I get to see every first moment of my children and give them all the love they need. Later on she did confess that she regrets not being able to stay at home with her children.*
>
> *Well, I went out to lunch, with my son in a comfy cloth carrier on my chest so he could hear my heartbeat. To get out, I took him on bike rides and walks and picnics and to parks to play with other children. And nobody's career ever said, I love you, Mommy.*

BE THE ROLE MODEL!

It is tough to defend your SAHM position and philosophy—so don't try. And, as I wrote earlier, don't bother with statistics or studies—that just provokes more anger and arguments. Just go on and on about both the challenges and the joys you've experienced. Talk about your relationship with your children and your husband, and how it's all gotten deeper and more touching now that you have more time and patience. Talk about how the life of a mom is not nine-to-five but twenty-four/seven, but that the immersion in family allows you to develop so many aspects of your being that even you are surprised. Talk about the adorable moments you've had with your kids, and describe each one vividly—that you were actually there to experience it will be an obvious point.

At times some critics will say, "It must be nice to just quit and take care of a kid all day"—as if there's no work in nursing, cleaning, and taking care of a child, without ever being able to leave and "go home." To them you should say, "Yes, it is nice—after all the housework is out of the way—to savor my children and my husband without the burden of having to throw off the workday at the office. You're right—it is nice."

Describing the best and the worst of the life you lead will give critics the flavor of your world—a tempting flavor, to be sure.

As one SAHM wrote,

I've had to defend my decision to be at home. My sister and sisters-in-law thought that I was taking the easy route by staying home. They thought it was a waste that I went to college and became an RN. They thought that I should have continued working and "contributed," so things wouldn't be so hard financially. I have come to realize that they were jealous.

They envied our dedication—but now they are all SAHMs!

Another SAHM wrote,

[All my critical college buddies] thought I was wasting all that I just learned by not continuing with my job. Funny thing is, now that they are all starting to have children, they have decided to stay home and do as I did—seeing that it was not as bad as they thought, and that my children have benefited by having me home.

That's what I'm talking about!

Summary Thought

I'd like to make your listeners aware of the International MOMS (Moms Offering Moms Sup-

port) Club. The MOMS Club is designed specifically for the stay-at-home moms by offering support during the daytime when moms need it most, in the form of play groups and other get-togethers. My local MOMS Club was a lifesaver, giving me a connection with other stay-at-home moms and something to do with my then two-year-old and newborn.

The best benefit was the support I got for my decision to stay home and raise my own kids. The dues for MOMS Club are nominal, about $30 for the year, and will be waived for those in financial need. For more information, or to find a local chapter, go to www.momsclub.org.

I can't say enough about how wonderful my experience was with these ladies, who five years later I count among my best friends.

4

HOW STAYING AT HOME IMPACTS THE MARRIAGE

Okay, now you've had a preface, an introduction, and three chapters that practically anoint you SAHMs with sainthood. This is the time to grab your heels and yank you back down to earth. While your efforts for the family are amazingly important, be careful you don't get an attitude that sounds a lot like this: "I'm stuck here all day with the kids, the laundry, and the dishes—I have to clean and do errands and take care of everything while you just go to work and come home and want to put your feet up and have me cater to you! You don't know how hard I work, and I don't think you show me any appreciation. Not only that—after the day I've had, you expect me to have sex? Are you kidding? I'm tired, and there is always so much more to do around this house while you sit around doing nothing."

Ouch!

If you take on the martyr/entitlement role, two things are definitely going to happen: you'll be a lot less happier with your life, and you will have a husband not exactly wanting to come home to you.

And then you have a SAHM whose point of view is profoundly different:

I am blessed to be loved by someone so remarkable. To this day—eighteen years later—he opens doors for me, tells me I'm the most beautiful woman he's ever seen, says I'm worth going through a little discomfort for anytime, ranging from the shower temperature to letting me put my ice cold feet on his very warm thighs; his eyes lighten and sparkle each time I ask how I look when getting ready to leave; he calls me every time he gets a few minutes away from his tasks at work; he fixes things around the house, yard, and cars; and he works very hard to ensure I can be at home with our children.

In turn, I allow him to be who he is; I cook his dinner; I freshen my face moments before he comes home, because in my mind we're still courting, though we're married with children; I tell him I love him, look forward to amorous interludes

with him, and tell him the things I like about him:
he's strong, handsome, smart, and a good father.
I'm so blessed to be his wife. He's a generous and
helpful neighbor, and he's a true and faithful war-
rior serving our country with honor . . . you know,
there's so much to see and appreciate.

Now those of you who are—admit it—acting like brats, wanting the attention and accolades without realizing that it goes two ways, need to learn that you get more love, attention, and appreciation by giving the same, not with demands or complaints.

Your husband comes home stressed too, you know. And he will be more available to romance you if you take care of him. I remind wives all the time on my radio program how simple it is to distract a man from his stress. One SAHM wrote,

Last night I think you would have been proud
of me! Really, I just did what you tell all of us
wives to do on a daily basis. My husband of five
years is stressed out with his job, as he is support-
ing me as a stay-at-home mom for our one, soon to
be two, children.

He hasn't been much fun to be around recently,
so after I put the one-year-old to bed last night,

I said, "Well, honey, why don't I help you relieve some of the stress?" He smiled.

I am not a very seductive woman normally, but I knew it was the right thing to do for him . . . even though I didn't "feel like it." Then it really dawned on me—being a "seductive woman" to my husband actually, amazingly, put ME in the mood too! Who knew?

It is a well-known phenomenon that happy husbands do household chores without being reminded. Take a note: you know how to make him happy.

TIME

Time is just not on the side of a two-career family. With both parents having jobs and careers, commuting, meetings, last-minute work disasters requiring immediate and prolonged attention, travel, workshops, phone calls, and e-mails, as well as the difficulties with so many employee and coworker personality and relationship issues, the mere act of coming home becomes yet another burden.

This is actually a very simple concept, as one SAHM wrote: "By staying at home I can rest when my baby rests, take care of my home and family, without feeling stressed or overworked. The result is I have more energy to love up my husband. This has strengthened our marriage beyond measure."

Homes, clothes, pets, kids, houseplants—and yourself—need to be cleaned and maintained. That takes time; and after a long day at work there isn't much enthusiasm left for preparing and consuming nutritious, home-cooked, family togetherness around the dinner table. Instead, there is a race to get "that family stuff" out of the way so you can go to bed. This is where a lot of arguments that disrupt family harmony are born, since the family is no longer the promised land of love, affection, contentment, and nurturance; no, instead it is yet another stress and strain, as each parent/spouse expects someone or something outside of themselves to take care of "that family stuff."

This "unisex" mentality of dueling careers, dueling hours, dueling responsibilities, and dueling realities may work for some people—I don't know who—but in reality, this much fragmentation of time and attention, and the requirement for all home responsibilities to be fifty-fifty, or else there is a fight and hell to pay, doesn't portend good things for a marriage or for the well-being of children.

With a SAHM, a family is less rushed about everything and anything. That's assuming, of course, that you're reasonably organized, you're not expecting everything to be perfect, and you don't put a ridiculous amount on your agenda to be done each day. I find those three aspects throw a large number of SAHMs to the curb. If you excessively push yourself, then the main purpose of being home is being sabotaged: you are "performing" rather than "living."

I am not most impressed by SAHMs who call me and tell me how hyper-organized and perfect everything in their home is. I am most impressed by SAHMs who call or write and tell me stories of endless hours spent with their children watching worms crawl or carpenters working on a nearby home, practicing blowing bubbles under water as their children learn to swim, teaching their children to help with the dinner place settings and how to stir the gooey fixings for corn bread, and getting ready to welcome Daddy home.

This is the living part that is so important for a high quality of life.

How does this all lead to a quality marital life? The more two people, a husband and wife, look forward to each other, to being home together and sharing tales about family; the more they turn to each other in troubled times, advise each other on problems, and look at each other as the main source of pleasure in life—well, obviously, the stronger the marriage.

It should come as no surprise to you that I suggest to SAHMs that they need to—brace yourself—actually catch a nap here and there when the kids are resting, so that at the end of the day they will not feel stressed or overworked. If you don't do that, you won't have the energy to actually enjoy your family and love up your husband.

Way too many families get way too caught up in having way too many activities per hour per day. Children do not need half a dozen sports, music, art, or theater activities. Kids actually need more free playtime without adult instruction and control. Play beautiful music in the home; go bike riding or ball playing with your children; give them art supplies and let 'em do their own thing. You don't have to pay or drive for children to experience the world and expand their horizons. They don't have to go to some special program to learn to plant a garden or take care of pets. Make these a typical part of your family experience. While they are engaged in these activities, you have the time to watch and/or get some chores done.

Remember, though, that a spotless, totally organized house is not necessarily the most warm, inviting, enjoyable, or appreciated place on the face of the earth. The warmth of a home comes from the attitude of the people in it, not the decor or the perfection of every detail. Think of your home as a magnet, and wonder what will most draw the human spirit to it.

MY DAY IS WORSE THAN YOURS . . . YOU OWE ME

Marriages are not strengthened by perpetually stressed-out spouses expecting the other to not ask for that "last straw": that last straw being anything from a hug, a conversation, a request, or a problem to be dealt with, to, ahem, sex! That "last straw" is a godsend . . . not to be seen as an imposition.

Dual-career marriages tend to be somewhat competitive and mutually demanding, even one-dimensional, mostly revolving around work, since work is the dominant aspect for both spouses. One newly converted SAHM explained,

> I think our marriage has improved greatly since I've become a SAHM. My husband and I used to work together. Our home lives revolved around business. Now that I'm no longer involved with the business, we have a bigger variety of topics to discuss (even if it's just what we did today and what Daddy missed while he was at work). I believe my husband respects me more. He sees a different side

of me; the softer, more nurturing side that didn't come out too much before having our daughter.

The competitive issue is no small one, involving everything from how much each makes each year to who did more chores around the house to who has more responsibilities, stress, and burdens. All too often, this just leads to arguments and animosity. When there is "division of labor," there's nothing to compete with. What one does to financially support the family is enjoyed by what the other does to take care of the family and build the home environment. Each feels like a "specialist" and has pride in his or her contribution— with each contribution of talents and efforts being seen as a gift rather than a fought-over task.

Now life is about sharing, rather than mutual demands. When husband and wife come together, each basking in the magnificence of their roles and their contribution to the family unit, they can talk about kids, dreams, goals, interests, problem-solving, and the love they have for each other.

I have often, when in private practice with couples, asked each in the presence of the other what they've done in the past forty-eight hours to make the other feel like a "man" or "woman." I generally get blank stares from each, sometimes simultaneously; both have lost that important sense of gender self because of their focus on career and general busyness. Years of feminism badgering both genders about their unique gender desires (as though they were faults or blemishes to be eradicated) have left both men and women confused and somewhat cautious about expressing what is natural to them: femininity and masculinity. When we lose that, we become worker ants rather than multidimensional human beings.

When a wife compliments her husband on his muscles, he's jazzed. When a husband compliments his wife on her tenderness, she's jazzed. We both need what is our birthright, and unisexuality is nobody's birthright—it is a mistaken notion derived from feminism's desire for equality. Equality is of value, not of substance. Water and food have equal value for survival, yet they are entirely different substances. Masculinity and femininity are of equal value—let us learn to respect and embrace the uniqueness of each.

OHHH, SEX

I realize that what I'm going to say next will dangle me above quicksand, but I believe it is a truth that needs to be said. In general, men's egos are best fed by protecting and providing, while women's egos are best fed by nurturing and caretaking. Men feel "manly" when they get to be the ones who slay the dragons. Women feel "womanly" when they get to be the ones in charge of the nest.

It is no accident that one of the best-remembered scenes in all of Hollywood's history is in the movie *Gone with the Wind*, when Scarlett is swept off her feet at the bottom of that long, high staircase, and carried up to the bedroom by her husband for a night of passion. Of course, as neurotic as she was, she ultimately could not admit to him that it made her feel more like a woman than ever before—but every other nonneurotic woman in the audience for decades felt it!

One of the more typical sad, marriage-ruining complaints from women is that they're not interested in sex. Sometimes their excuse—or explanation—is that they've been scarred by some childhood "molestation" that they never informed their husbands about before marriage, or never worked through therapeutically before the nuptials, but generally it's that there is just too much to do with a full-time job, part-time this, or other-time that, and some kids and a house to boot. The thought that they have a moral and loving commitment to be sexual with their husbands (and have a good time doing so) makes 'em angry and determined to call *Ms.* magazine and report me as a traitor to those with mammary glands!

Sex, as I've said earlier, is an incredible gift from God and nature, and to turn down the bonding, exciting, loving, and downright horny aspect of your life because you're so busy, busy, busy is, frankly, seriously stupid.

IT'S WAY TOO MUCH ABOUT THE KIDS

While the time and effort and exhaustion inherent in having and raising children are realities, care must be taken not to make those children the center of the universe, with no orbiting planets. The most important nurturing and caretaking aspect of child-rearing is a quality marriage as the backdrop. The problems people call me with in their adult relationships generally have to do with mimicking their original family's behaviors: how Mom and Dad treated each other becomes either a buoy under them, helping them have quality relationships, or an anchor around their legs, pulling them down into the abyss of relationship chaos.

This means that if you two ignore the primary husband-wife love relationship, almost no amount of schmoozing with kids is going to replace what they've lost in not learning from Mom and Dad about how to maintain love in the midst of the stresses of life.

Admittedly, this is a difficult transition. Before kids, the two of you had little distractions from being a couple (unless one of you was neurotically and overly invested in childish things like four hours of video games each night, or inappropriate things like the dramas of your original biological family); but after children come on the scene, well, those dependent little creatures are virtual tyrants, demanding every ounce of attention and strength you have. It is easy to see how a husband and wife can drift apart when their heads seem to be perpetually turned toward the children.

Thinking, "Well, that's okay for now; it won't last forever," is a deadly plan. Once people start going on parallel paths, the paths often start diverging and may intersect other paths (uh-oh) where attention is more forthcoming, or just seem to dissipate, like smoke rising from an ember. It is much easier to maintain than try to re-create.

So do everything you can to maintain your relationship: cuddle together with the kid(s), have Grandma babysit each weekend so that you can have a date night to play, make sure each day and night you make sweet contact with each other through thought, word, deed, and touch, and say sweet somethings to each other every night before you drift off to a well-earned sleep.

Not making these efforts actually undermines what you are trying to do with staying home for the children, since then the primary relationship won't be the parental one—as it should.

It is important to note that the focus on the children must be a mutual one, not one in which one dominates and the other takes a back seat. I see too many circumstances where one parent, most often the mom, decides that only she knows what is best, how and what should be or not be done, and so forth, leaving the father of the children, and her supposedly beloved husband, almost totally out of the picture. I've heard women complain that their husbands are too tough with disciplining and such, and I've had to explain the different, but mutually necessary, modes of mothering and fathering.

For instance, when a toddler falls down, Mommy is right there, kissing the boo-boo and wiping the tears and cuddling the distressed little body. When a toddler falls down and it is Daddy right there, he checks to make sure no bone is broken or artery exposed, lifts the kid right back on his feet, tells him he is fine, and sends him off to continue interacting with the world. The mother offers comfort; the father stimulates stoicism. Both aspects are equally necessary. Too many moms go into a "Dad is mean" mode in their minds and put their husbands down.

More "mothering" books and magazines have to focus on the absolutely necessary polarity of masculinity and femininity in raising children. Unless a woman fully understands this, her nurturing will be the only aspect a child will focus on, and her relationship with her man will be destroyed.

I often tell mothers either to let their children handle the problem, or to send in Dad to help them learn to risk more, so they can survive better in a life with perpetual challenges. It's nice to know Mommy is there for a mommy hug and mommy power—but Dad's input is absolutely essential for balance. Without that balance, kids never learn to feel and to be confident.

If you take on the SAHM role, it doesn't mean that the kids are your turf exclusively, and the children should know very clearly that you and their dad are a united front. This makes life clearer and easier for the children, and prevents them from playing one of you off against the other, so that one of you seems like the good/loving one, while the other is the enemy; this will destroy the children, the family, and the marriage.

R-E-S-P-E-C-T

It should be obvious also that, as with every "team," focus on a mutual goal is the glue that holds the team together. When someone on the team acts independently, wanting to stand out as the "star," the team suffers. It's good to nurture the sense that while you and your husband both have different roles in the family and with the children, the well-being of the children and the family is your shared goal.

And as you notice on the baseball, football, basketball, and other fields, when one does something especially triumphant for the team, everybody else jumps up and down and hugs and high-fives them and each other. Keep that in mind when a kid does something special, Mom makes a great budget, or Dad gets kudos at work: it is all for the team, and the team should celebrate whenever any of its members accomplish something. This is where competition, even between siblings, much less between parents, is eradicated, and a loving sense of intimate bonding is put in its place.

Going back to the concept of competitiveness between spouses—reminiscent of sibling rivalry and "you owe me"—it is vital that respect be demonstrated for Mom and Dad's contributions. Respect is much more than a thank-you. Respect requires you to be contemplative in quiet moments about how important each and every effort is that the other puts into all the relationships, work, and maintenance that make a family function well, creating peace, contentment, joy, and happiness for each family member, leading to each member's ability to function in the world with confidence and courage.

If you are too busy to notice other than your own efforts, you miss out on an essential opportunity to appreciate what is solid and caring in your life. If your husband took two minutes to wipe the ice off your windshield, that should warm your heart and help you appreciate him more every time he does some small thing to make your life better. Perhaps you could flip the switch on the automatic coffeemaker so that when he walks into that kitchen, he can "smell the coffee" and know you thought of him.

While these small things are the biggest cornerstone of a loving relationship, it is ultimately the respect you feel and acknowledge that demonstrate your maturity. Immaturity leads people to constantly measure their importance and pump it up, even at the expense of their loving spouses—or sometimes their own children! Maturity allows you to be more accepting of your own abilities and limitations, and to relish what is special in others, especially your spouse and children.

Every man who has had a SAHM knows how magnificent and important such a woman has become to the family and to the world. Men who have grown up with career women, nannies, day care, and babysitters haven't had this experience and often discount the value or necessity of a SAHM. I would not recommend that a woman choose such a man—but many women have had the same background and come late to the beautiful reality of a SAHM, having already married a "liberated man."

These transitions can be painful; I generally recommend that such a wife bring her husband to meet other husbands of SAHMs to get past their defensiveness (as in, protecting and defending how they were brought up) or their selfishness ("I want two checks so I can have an expensive lifestyle with lotsa toys!").

Perhaps SAHM groups should start a Dad-at-Work Anonymous organization to help these husbands reclaim their masculine birthright to protect and provide. When men rebel against the SAHM concept, I believe it is their defensiveness, as I've explained, as well as a lack of respect for their own masculinity.

One SAHM explained how her marriage has benefited:

> My husband feels good, knowing that he can financially support us and that his wife prefers to raise his child rather than have a job. I am happy, which of course makes my husband happy. Even

though we have separate responsibilities, we have really grown to respect each other for what the other one brings to the marriage. We have a greater appreciation for the other person.

When my husband has to work late or is under a deadline, it makes me think of how much I love and need him, and how he really works so hard for us and how he does all this with gratitude! Also, on the occasions when he looks after our daughter, he is always amazed and appreciative of how hard my job is. I am so lucky to have him and couldn't do this without him.

MY HUSBAND IS MY BEST FRIEND

I was quite touched to read an e-mail from a woman who said just that: "My husband is now my best friend." She explained that her marriage has changed dramatically since she decided to be a SAHM: "We are closer because I am taking care of his needs much better than I was able to when I was working. My respect for him has doubled now that he is the primary wage earner. His confidence in himself is higher now also."

This is the perspective of a woman who appreciates the feminine reality that men do better and are better when they're taken care of by a good woman. That's just a fact of nature.

As I've said, men are like water pumps; they need to be primed, and then the good stuff flows back at you.

Another woman wrote to me that now that she's at home, her family can go on a lot of trips and enjoy the weekends because they aren't catching up on laundry, housecleaning, grocery shopping, and so on. "My husband is relieved of doing any housework, so he can relax at night and spend time with the kids. He works really hard during the day and is tired when he gets home, so I am glad to make him dinner and let him relax. I don't resent him, whereas I think I would if I were working and doing all the housework too. It's my job to take care of the home and meals, and we share child-rearing. We have a GREAT life, and I know that would not be the case if I was working out of the home."

Another mother described the deeper love and respect she has for her husband since becoming a SAHM. She sees what he does day after day so that she can stay home with their daughter, and she appreciates the sacrifices he's made transitioning from his former childless life. He continually tells her how happy he is that she is home and how much he appreciates her for doing this for them . . . for them! She thought it strange that he would thank her continually for being home raising their child, because she wouldn't have had it any other way—so no sacrifice there! "When he tells me he loves me, there is a difference from before; I know he loves me the way he did when we didn't have our daughter, but there is another love that only comes from witnessing what you do for your children for love."

Wow! I have always said that the sexiest thing about a husband to a good wife is watching him play with their children. See? That goes two ways!

Summary Thought

I could not have a marriage if I were working, or probably even if I were trying to work part-time and raise my toddler. I wouldn't be able to take care of the house the way I do. My husband would not have a warm meal and a warm smile waiting for him when he gets home from work. And I definitely would not have the energy to be a babe at night (can you tell I have read The Proper Care and Feeding of Marriage*?).*

Although he struggles with his new career, considering how much he loved teaching, I know that he feels a sense of pride and meaning that he is supporting the healthy childhood of our son. He is a champion of the family. Being able to stay at home with our son means that I have the mental capacity and physical energy (however minimal on some days!) to be his WIFE and not just a live-in housekeeper.

Not that we don't have difficulties. I have struggled with depression and anxiety through the process of becoming a mother, as he has in the process of becoming a father and the only wage-earner. I think raising kids in general puts a huge strain on a marriage, maybe even more so if both parents have radically changed their lives so one parent can stay home. All of that considered, though, I truly believe that our commitment to have me stay at home, and the team effort of making that happen, has strengthened our bond and love despite the sacrifices.

—a stay-at-home mom

5

HOW STAY-AT-HOME MOMS BENEFIT KIDS

I remember a few years back getting a slew of ferocious mommy mail. It seems that *Sesame Street* had begun an ongoing "kids in day care" subplot, which, according to the SAHMs, seriously encouraged children to prefer day care to their own homes with their own mommies.

Moms still write me, frazzled that their kids seem to think they are missing out on something because so many of their friends go to day care. One complained,

My older daughter asked how come she can't go to KIDS club (after-school day care) like her friends do. I have to constantly explain that her friends have mommies who work. I tell her that her friends would much rather be at home with

their mommies, playing games, cuddling, etc. Instead, their mommies pick them up late, have to rush home to make dinner and/or pick up fast food, do homework, take baths, etc. They don't have a lot of quality time to spend with their children.

Wow! SAHMs are now on the defensive for taking care of their little ones? Since when did raising your own children become something you have to defend or feel guilty for?

Another quite frustrated SAHM wrote,

Recently I had an argument with my sister about my children not going to a day care. She feels that I am neglecting my children by not sending them to one. I told her that I had children so that I could be their mom—not some other woman or man! I also told her that by not sending them, I am keeping them safe from neglect, abuse, and molestation.

She ended the conversation with, "You are not socializing your kids, and that is wrong." Today I received a phone call from my mother backing my sister! I interrupted my mother to tell her that I was not wrong for keeping my kids safe at home and would continue to do so.

First of all, "neglect"? Where do you see neglect when a mother is there for her baby's every waking and sleeping moment, tending to all the child's needs? Second of all, "socialization"? What little socialization infants engage in needs to be with their mommy—not some other infant. Children nurtured by a loving, attentive parent must have an advantage over kids "raised" by other kids—remember the movie *Lord of the Flies*? There was a situation where peers dominated over adult supervision and earlier moral training; the children became vicious amoral animals.

The fact is, a mommy can take a child to parties, the park, or relatives' and friends' homes and "socialize" all that is necessary and healthy for any child.

One SAHM was sitting in her six-month-old daughter's pediatrician's office, leafing through the books on the table. She had begun reading a section in one of the books, about the changes and challenges of the coming months of a child's development, when she came upon the following: "Make sure other people who provide care and supervision for your baby understand the importance of forming a loving and comforting relationship with your child."

This mom wrote me that she read it ten times because she just couldn't believe it!

"Other people" and "loving and comforting" your child seemed kind of contradictory. I can just imagine a mom appearing at day care with a list of values she'd like the day-care staff to instill: "Don't forget honesty and kindness . . . and be sure to be loving. Now, bye, I have to go to work."

I suppose we all have different priorities, but forming a good, loving, and comforting relationship with my child is my responsibility and obligation, not something I can simply pass off to "other people."

And when you do pass it off to "other people," they become "Mommy." One recent radio caller had that very problem. It seems that she worked some five hours a day, with commuting added to that time, and her mother had taken care of her child every day from the time her child was three months old. Her child naturally gravitated to the grandma whenever they were all together, because that had been the child's source of love, cuddling, nurturing. Just like a duckling that follows anything it considers its mother, human babies are drawn to the actual "motherer."

My advice was to tank the part-time job and reclaim the one with her child, understanding, of course, that there will be an emotionally difficult transition time while the child's sense of security and attachment switch over.

HIRED HELP AS MOMMY?

Does anybody really really really really believe that you can pay hired help to really love a child? Really?

One ex-child-care worker answered that question for me. She wrote that she was a preschool teacher in a day-care center before she became a mother. She thought she loved all the kids as though they were hers. They did seem hers in a way, because she spent more time with them than their parents spent; she played with them, kissed their boo-boos, gave them snacks and lunch, changed their diapers, and rocked them to sleep for their naps.

When she later became a mother, she realized that she never had loved those children; she liked them a lot and enjoyed her job. Mostly, thinking back, she felt sorry for them. When she became a mother, she instantly felt the difference, in that she really, truly loved her child. "Nobody," she wrote, "nobody could ever LOVE my child and take care of him the way I do—NOBODY EVER!"

Now that is testimony from someone caretaking, sweet, responsible, and kind. And—it's also the truth. Nobody—ever—will love your children like you would . . . unless your ability to love is compromised by some assortment of emotional problems.

One e-mail writer described growing up in a household where both parents always worked. She remembered all the times she spent alone as a latchkey kid, sometimes even making her own dinners as a rather young child. From her perspective, her parents were so wrapped up in their careers and jobs that they weren't there to guide, support, and frankly, nag her. Consequently, she was never encouraged or pushed in her schoolwork or any kind of outside interest. Her parents were generally unaware of what was going on in her life. Of course, at the time, she thought that was quite normal. But now, from the perspective of an adult, she believes that if one of her parents had had the time to consistently devote to her and her life, it would have drastically lessened the many struggles she had to go through as a young adult.

Because of her personal experience without a SAHM, she has committed herself to being one. Her answer to the question "How do you think your child is impacted by having a SAHM?" is "Ask my child in fifteen years, when she is a happy, secure adult"— without, perhaps, a lot of the chaos, confusion, and excessive inappropriate experimentation that comes when kids are not primarily bonded to their parents and lack loving, involved supervision.

One of my listeners related that she'd planned to put her nineteen-month-old baby in day care so she could go back to work. To be quite honest, she just wanted more money to be able to do and buy more things. She found a good job opportunity that was to begin in two weeks, so the drive to get the day-care thing going was strong. She and her husband checked out twenty establishments to find a suitable day care.

> *I visited at least twenty of these "facilities," and I must tell you how shocked and saddened I was by my experience. I can't tell you how many I walked into, and the little two- and three-year-olds who could talk would say, "My mommy's coming to get me," with little distraught looks on their faces. Or, "When is my mommy coming?" I can't tell you how sad it made me feel to see these kids in these centers with no real love—only put there as a means for their parents to do something else besides being their child's parent.*

Her decision then was to stay home with their son. She and her son continue to go to the 10:00 AM story time at the library; she teaches him his ABCs, sings songs to him, dances with him, and most importantly, gives him all of the hugs and kisses he could ever need. She is there to guide his little steps as he grows into a man. She will teach him manners, morals, and how to be a good person. Obviously, no one else could ever do that exactly the way she can . . . she's his mommy.

"It's been over a year, and I can't get the image of this little day-care boy out of my mind," wrote a listener.

> I was leaving a grocery store when two day-care workers each rolled a ten-child stroller across the parking lot and into the day-care center. Just as the final stroller was pulled through the door, I glanced up to meet the eyes of a shy, adorable youngster. At most, he was two, as were all the "cargo" of unsmiling, unhappy-looking kids.
>
> I was about to get into my car when he suddenly broke into a frown, threw his little arms toward me, and cried out, "MOMMY!" in the most heart-wrenching voice—and then he started crying. The dour worker glared at me and disappeared with her brood into the day-care center.
>
> Dr. Laura, I don't particularly like children; I'm fifty-five and childless. But at that moment, all your preaching, teaching, and nagging about the

choice of child care versus at-home parenting really pushed my empathy button.

I remembered the confusion and angst I felt as a nine-year-old when my mom made the decision to go to work to help my dad pay the bills. We were responsible kids, my brother and I, but the emptiness and abandonment are still tangible today.

I believe that her choice helped cement the deep-down sense of unlovability I've carried all my life, and that has influenced the negative choices that have so hurt my life for so long. Please keep banging the drum for the moms who love enough to stay home with their children. We children DO remember . . . even across the decades.

It's hard to imagine that it doesn't matter to children whether or not they're herded by a nanny, day-care worker, or babysitter, or cuddled by mommy.

ANGRY B**CH BEGONE!

One newly converted SAHM wrote, "I was now not a stressed-out, angry b**ch, constantly yelling at her kids out of frustration and impatience."

I've heard that admission from a lot of moms! I'm really quite pleased they admit these unfortunate emotions to me, because venting to someone who'll support them to discover their better selves is a good thing!

A recent caller told me that she was concerned that she is pretty mean with her husband and her child over mostly "petty" things. Her response to my question "Why do you think you are so on edge all the time?" was that she has three children, all under the age of three (imagine!). When queried as to what might set her off, she replied, "When they play and make too much noise." I just had the strong feeling that there was more to the story than simply having the three little ones so close in age.

I pushed again with, "What was your childhood like?" She responded that she had to be the good child, quiet and compliant, because her mother had so much trouble controlling her brother. I suggested to her that she never really had a normal, playful childhood, and she resented her children for seemingly having what she was kept from.

The example I gave was silly, but it hit the spot with her: "Imagine not being allowed to eat ice cream, and watching all the other kids licking, slurping, and dripping piled-high strawberry ice-cream cones . . . you'd feel resentment, wouldn't you?"

She got it. I suggested she take the older child—as the two others were napping—and sit on the floor, either digging their hands into a huge bowl of Jell-O or having a fake whipped cream fight (less calories), and allow herself this second opportunity to be playful "with" her kids, if not "as" a kid.

Happily, she sounded receptive to the concept of getting in touch with her playful, childlike part and her needs to let go and enjoy!

The point of all of this is that just being there is not enough. Sometimes you may have to do what it takes to throw off some of the rotten stuff from your own childhood that prevents you from approaching motherhood with an open, calm heart and the stamina to withstand the obvious stresses and strains of taking care of little ones. And, as I've said in an earlier chapter, sometimes trying to be too perfect is its own impediment to enjoying your child and your life.

If you find yourself short-tempered and impatient, stop and think about dropping everything else, just getting down in the sandbox, and having a good time with your kids—those emotional memories are the most important for your children and, frankly, for you.

After I suggested to a stressed-out SAHM caller on my program that she get an iPod and fill it with the music she most loves (for me it would be oldies rock) and carry it on her person all the time save for showers, sleeping, and sex, so she can turn it on and have the music lift her spirits while she dances around, I received the following from a SAHM-to-be:

Your iPod advice really works! A month or so ago I realized I had been taking out my stress on my five-year-old collie. Our walks had turned into me dragging her around the neighborhood by the collar. I scolded her for normal dog behavior—like when she got bouncy when I returned home from the store.

I am a SAHM-to-be (our baby is due in two months) and was having a hard time transitioning from a stressful, take-charge job to being dependent on my husband's income. Even knowing how fortunate I am that I do not have to work, I just felt so out of control.

My pregnancy hormones did not make the situation any better. One day I cried after seeing her sweet face get all scrunched up like I was going to hit her while I scolded her for some small thing. I felt terrible! What an unfit parent I was turning into! I heard your iPod advice on the radio and decided to try it immediately. It works! Now I listen to my iPod when I start to feel a little overwhelmed, and always walk my dog with it. My

*husband even mentioned that I was transitioning
really well. As I write this, my dog is curled up at
my feet. Thank you so much for your advice—you
restored sanity to a deranged pregnant woman.*

What do they say about music's charms?

The main point is, just being there is necessary
but not sufficient. You need to be able to give of
yourself to an extraordinary degree without experiencing massive burnout, resentments, hostilities, and
so forth. That means you may have to have an attitude adjustment, some quickie techniques of releasing
stress (music, fifteen minutes of lovin' with your husband before bedtime, yoga, and so on), and a willingness to simply enjoy the experience of watching your
little one develop. One day they can't walk, the next
day they're running. One day they can't talk, the
next day they won't stop. Everything they see, smell,
hear, and do is a new miracle—enjoy the ride, even
though the house isn't perfect and your neighbor has
more jewelry.

SAHM AS SURROGATE MOM

It is curious that so many two-career families have
expressed so much appreciation for the rare SAHM

in the neighborhood who drives their kids home from school at the normal time, and lets them play at her home until the two-career parents leave work and make it to their houses. Clearly, the appreciation must signal that they recognize some benefit in a warm home to come to with cookies and milk, a kind smile, time to share, safety, and comfort.

My children definitely like me being there for them and their needs. They like that I know their friends and their friends like me. For those friends whose parents are working, I become the "surrogate mom," taking them for an ice cream, to the mall, etc. I also give my kids' friends rides home from school. The children really like that extra time away from school to spend with their friends, and I use the time to stay acquainted with their friends. I do not know how parents cannot feel compelled to know with whom their children are interacting. I do know the working moms whose children play with mine are grateful to me for taking in their children and treating them as family. I like it that other moms and kids can count on me to be there for the safety of all the kids, not just my own.

Besides, I think kids are fun!

KIDS LOVE HOME AND HEARTH AND MOM

When asked what benefit a SAHM provides to her children, one mother wrote,

> *My children are secure in who they are. I see the benefits of me being home with them on a daily basis. Even in the simpleness of picking them up from school and hearing them sing as they leave the cares of school behind them and come home to a warm, welcome, safe place where they know that I will be. Always. I think they have felt that they can count on the consistency. They know that they will always have a warm and safe place to land.*
>
> *They know that if they throw up at school, I will be there to come pick them up and have a blanket and a bowl ready, as well as their favorite video and lots of snuggles. My kids love that I am able to come and help out at school; that I will always come to any play, poem, or project that occurs. They are sure of themselves, as they have their love tanks filled to the brim on a daily basis, and they know beyond a shadow of a doubt not only that am I home, but that their daddy and I love each other and them with a passion.*

One mother who didn't decide to be a SAHM until the birth of her second child, got the following question from her eight-year-old son: "Mom, how much time does the president get to spend with his family?" His mommy answered, "I'm sure he wants to spend a lot of time with them, but because he is so important to our country and has such a huge job, he probably doesn't get to spend very much time with his wife and children."

Her son was quiet for a while, as though he was thinking about something else, but spoke up again to say, "Well, Mom, I don't want to be president. My wife and kids will be more important. They'll need me around."

It is amazing that such a young child can understand the principle of ambition being trumped by priorities, obligations, and choices.

Children are minors for only eighteen years—after that, every parent is free and clear to chase any dream or fantasy that the marriage can accommodate. There is no reason that parents can't work around their family's schedule and personal needs to take on hobbies, part-time endeavors, schooling, and so forth. It hopefully seems reasonable that children and family should not be pushed aside for personal ambitions; however, some personal ambitions can readily be experienced in the context of family and children when the two parents work together—dividing time and involvement—and keeping up the loving bonds with the gift of time, attention, and priority.

THE SWEETEST MOMENTS

The best way to clarify to you how much it means to children to have you at home with them is to tell you stories. One mother wrote that she and her daughter had a girls' day out, and during this outing, the daughter told her that her friends told her that she was lucky because their moms don't do that with them. She said that one girl even asked her mom if they could spend Saturday together, and the mom told her that she works all week and Saturday is the only day she has for herself, and she wasn't going to spend it running around with her daughter; she was going to spend it doing what she wanted to do, which was nothing! The SAHM said that her daughter described the other little girl as very hurt.

"The children told us that they would never let us go to a nursing home; that they would take care of us when we get old because we have taken care of them. Of course, no parent wants their child taking care of them when they are old, for many reasons, but it is nice to know that through our actions, we have instilled in our children the importance of family," she continued.

Many parents have written me to point out that having a SAHM is a benefit to a child for so many reasons. The child is very attached to the parent and doesn't have to misbehave or "act out" to get attention—the attention is a given. Having a SAHM means that finances are probably stretched—but believe it or not, that can be a very good thing for a family, as one SAHM pointed out:

> The impact on our children is significant. Because of our single-income situation, we have to watch our pennies. We can't hire out gardening or yard work, housecleaning, etc. We do it all. We were able to purchase a century-old home on a half acre where our kids can play and ride their various wheeled items. They also work in the yard with Dad every week and help clean the house. We ALL do yard work AND housework. The three oldest can use tools, fix things, paint, strip wallpaper, and many other things under the tutelage of Grandpa and Grandma, who "winter" with us six months out of the year. They are dropped off and picked up or walk to and from school, depending upon age. I am there to make healthy homemade

meals and to help with homework. We eat dinner together as a family, sometimes squished around our table. Their friends are always welcome in our home, and we closely monitor where they go and who they are with. They are part of a team and understand that it takes all of us to make this household and family run.

This could not have come to be if I were still working full-time. The benefits are tremendous and keep on making themselves manifest. I cannot imagine it any other way!

Another SAHM told me that her three children, twelve, fourteen, and sixteen, have thanked her for being home and homeschooling them. She describes them as usually extremely loving and respectful, pointing out that good relationships take time. She is convinced that most of the rudeness that is considered normal these days would go away with more family time and less focus on money and achievement.

Some parents who put their newborns and toddlers in day care say it is for their own good; that they learn independence. One SAHM countered, "Independence comes from knowing who we are and feeling secure; not from booting the little birds out of the next before they are ready to fly."

The best observations about the impact of SAHMs on children come not from studies and research; nope, the best observations come from the experiment of not having been home and then switching:

> My son has been the real beneficiary of my becoming a SAHM. All his life was relegated to others taking care of him, not having his mom around to raise him, having family members step in and do what I should have done.
>
> He handled it all so well, never complained when he had to be shipped off to another location or do things he didn't want to do. It was the greatest gift to give him when I told him I would be home all the time to take care of him. He became less stressed, happier, calmer, and more loving. He could actually have a childhood with friends, play dates, and join things if he wanted to. I will never regret staying home. Wish I could have done it sooner, but it's never too late to make your child your priority and to be a real mom.

One SAHM wrote that when she did consider going back to work and she and her husband discussed it with their daughter, "She cried. She had been used to me being there since she was born, and I think she felt as though I was abandoning her. That basically said it all for me."

Yet another SAHM convert wrote that her son is much happier having her at home, not as "needy" for her, and he started sleeping through the night shortly after she started staying home. Prior to her staying home, he was up every hour to hour and a half. The best compliment they receive about their son is how happy he is, and his mom attributes that to both of them being there for him and putting him first in their lives, not fitting him into their lives.

One adorable note from a SAHM started out with, "As I type this my one-year-old and three-year-old are climbing around on me . . . so I think they like having their mother around."

I am not recording any more of what she said— because I think this says it all!

Summary Thought

I try to listen as often as I can in my car when I go to pick up my kids from school at 1:30 PM Pacific Time. I live in Tijuana, Baja California, and I am excited to learn that no matter where you live, the same moral standards are espoused.

I especially support the comments that when you choose to be a mom, you have to be 100 percent there for the kids. And I try to explain to my six-year-old girl that it doesn't matter if her cousins have a bigger house, a brand-new car, designer clothes, and their mom is an executive who works from seven to seven. BUT, the bond we have NO money can buy. Felicidades for all your comments! No matter if you're American, Anglo, Latin . . . we all NEED to have the same MORAL TRUTHS so we can have a better world.

Sincerely, Yolanda C. G.

6

BEING A STAY-AT-HOME MOM CHANGES YOU

While I thought nine months of pregnancy—during the first three of which morning sickness made it impossible to eat, while the last three made bowel movements difficult—culminating in a twelve-hour labor resulting in an error-ridden epidural and C-section, and then a painfully injected blood patch to stop my cerebrospinal fluid from leaking, was the major test of my grit to be a mommy, let alone a SAHM . . . I discovered that all of that was only the entrance exam!

When the hospital pediatric nurses hand you your baby for breast-feeding, the babies all seem to be quiet, relaxed, cuddly, and hungry. Be sure to read the small print on the paperwork they give you when go home with your child, because there are "hints" that the baby's demeanor will probably be different once you get home. I didn't believe them. From the moment we all got home, he began to cry, and for the life of me, I couldn't figure out what the problem was and how to comfort him. You get advice from all sorts of people about driving around in the car (not so great an idea when you're already too tired to keep your own eyes open), rocking chairs (I loved them), hot water bottles (oh, that wasn't for my back?), music (perhaps acid rock isn't the best choice? . . . just kidding!), and so on. Well, nothing worked. And I discovered that I did not have the magic to simply make my baby happy and comfortable 100 percent of the time.

To a woman who is used to conquering projects and challenges that are tests of my physical or mental abilities, this experience of not knowing what was going on and what I was supposed to do about it was so unbelievably frustrating that I felt incompetent, stupid, and somewhat lost . . . never mind scared that I was going to be one lousy mommy.

He would never nap for long, crying was continuous, and I was getting strained past all imagination. One early evening I happened to see one of those throwaways that fill up your mailbox: it showed a picture of a stuffed bear next to a sleeping baby, and that caught my attention. I read about the "Heart Bear," a stuffed animal that had a nine-volt battery-driven continuous tape of the mother's heartbeat as heard from the womb by the fetus. When my husband came home from work, I desperately waved the advertisement and said, "Find this bear—and don't come home without it!" Sorry, that's the state of mind of a recently postpartum mother with a perpetually crying baby.

Some hours later my husband returned with the Heart Bear! He'd found it at Best Buy, which happened to be open late. I anxiously plugged in the battery, turned it up full blast, heard the rhythmic thumping that every child hears when inside Mommy, and to my amazement, watched my son's eyes first get wide, then snap shut as he went off to never-never land. Wow! What a lifesaver!

With that hint, I would have him nap on my chest while I lay on my back, and I carried him everywhere in a cloth carrier that held him up against my chest. While I love even the memory of those delicious moments, it also meant that cutting the umbilical cord at birth was only symbolic; becoming a new mommy meant that everything you wished to do, including go to the bathroom or take a shower, depends upon the tyrannical whim of something that weighs 5 percent of what you weigh, can't talk, can't walk, and can't change channels or dial up the Internet.

The first feelings most SAHMs go through are the helplessness of not knowing what the baby needs and wants at each moment, the frustration of being out of control of the situation, and the profound loss of any amount of independence. Suddenly work, with its lunch and coffee breaks, starts looking grand! And then your baby smiles up at you, and gently touches your face, exploring every nook and cranny of your eyes, nose, mouth, and cheeks; then you're hooked in again; but only for a while, because those feelings just keep getting recycled from hour to hour or day to day.

You come to learn a lot about yourself—good and bad—and you spend more time maturing more quickly than you ever have before. I know that I understand more about myself and the world, and about sacrifice, than I ever thought about before. Being a mom, especially a SAHM, is a sacrifice of incredible dimensions and a real test of your ability to give (the never-ending variety), endure, postpone gratification, think of somebody else way, way above yourself from moment to moment, be patient beyond reason, and have a sense of humor and a willingness to admit to weakness, ignorance, need, exhaustion, and nuttiness.

All of that and more—punctuated by seemingly endless cycles of diaperings and feedings.

JOY IN CHANGING DIAPERS, CLEANING TOILETS, AND COOKING DINNER?

In the military, latrine and KP duties are generally not considered promotions. Folks you may hire to clean your bathrooms, cook your meals, or iron your clothes are usually earning the minimum wage. In view of these facts, it's easy to imagine how dealing with the relentless needs of a new child (especially if you already have others) in addition to taking care of duties that are not highly esteemed can be a big downer to one's ego, one's sense of self-worth, and one's self-perceived value to the family. These feelings often lead a SAHM to badger her husband, demanding that he do housework so that she doesn't feel like the slave or the unpaid help. These feelings often mean there is no enjoyment in being a mother at all—and that is a great sadness.

What I've discovered is that it's all about perspective. If you choose to look at doing these housekeeping necessities as drudgery, then you'll feel lousy about it. If you choose to look at doing these housekeeping necessities as a clear and present means of giving—of showing your love of and for family—then you'll feel pooped at the end of the day . . . but you'll also feel immense satisfaction and inner warmth.

"I learned that it's the most incredibly satisfying thing in the universe to pour your life into your family and see what you've created . . . that no one else would ever be in the position to do . . . and to decide to do it well," wrote one three-decade SAHM. She ended her letter saying that she wished she could grab hold of every young woman, married or not, look deep into her eyes, and tell her, "There could never be a more incredible privilege than to be the heart of your home!"

Many of you reading this book have been quite independent women raised with the mantra, "If you are not working at a paying job, you are a slacker—at best!" Because of this brainwashing, you probably never saw being a SAHM as a viable or valuable "job," since you wouldn't be leaving the home each day to earn a paycheck—that tangible reward for and indication of your importance and your efforts.

Many women discover, as they become SAHMs, that hugs, smiles, dirty faces, laughter, kisses, adoring glances, and such mean so much more to you—even though you're still afraid to admit that to your feminista friends and relatives, lest they scoff at your newly found "simpleminded" ways.

Frankly, one of the greatest blessings in life is to learn to be content with and fulfilled by the small, simple things in life; after all, these make up the majority of the human experience.

Of course, these "simpleminded ways" come with a price: you'll feel like you're always nursing, changing diapers, soothing away tears, bathing baby, rocking in a chair to get baby to sleep for a few blessed moments; and in truth, that *is* all you'll be doing for a while. Then you get to have conversations and walk hand in hand, experiencing everyday life—which, because your child is discovering it for the first time, takes the banal to the amazing. It is a blast realizing that every day you're watching your child grow into a unique human being . . . and that you have the greatest influence on what kind of person he'll become.

I'M BETTER THAN I THOUGHT!

It is ironic that some women, strict and ferocious feministas at one time in their lives, who then "give in," marry, and then—oh my gosh—become SAHMs, discover that they are so incredibly tenderhearted and patient with their children—more than they were before the baby came. What has happened is that they've gotten in touch with their feminine side—something that being a feminista "protects" you from.

I am better at home crafts than I ever thought possible. I can sew, cook, clean, and make beautiful things for my home. I have learned how to keep plants alive in vegetable and flower gardens as well as random places around my yard.

[Because of these talent discoveries] I have gained confidence, when before I thought that the only way to gain confidence was through working outside the home or going to college. I do have a BA degree, and plan to go back for my MA someday. But I now know that these tools are not always what makes a woman successful.

This response, from a SAHM who obviously surprised herself by increasing her range of talents and outlets for creativity, is one that I hear quite often. It seems a tremendous revelation to many women that they can expand their horizons more as a SAHM than as a worker bee on someone else's schedule, using only certain required abilities.

What many women discover is who they really are. When we women spend all our time excelling at school and excelling at work, we sometimes get to the point of feeling neutered; we aren't women, with all the sensitivity and sensuality that entails. This often results in difficulties when transitioning into SAHMhood; we experience depression faced with the boredom and loneliness of being home every day, not having specific and accepted ways of proving our worth on a daily basis—or so we think.

It often takes women a while to shift out of the depression enough to discover the much more far-reaching and positive impact a woman can have as the center, the focal point, the lifeblood of the family.

The major issue of this transition is, I believe, one of the most important tasks of maturation; that is, becoming less self-centered. Being responsible for children, a home, and a husband teaches you to live outside yourself, for something and someone other than yourself.

Getting accolades, applause, bonuses, and such is great—I love 'em too! It's just that the ultimate quality of your life is not in your résumé but in the minds and hearts of those you mean something to because you gave of yourself to them.

"What I learned about myself is to be confident in what I believe in, no matter what everyone else in the world thinks or does nowadays," was the comment of a SAHM listener who was clearly rebelling against the modern-day notion that hired help trumps Mama. Many women have called me, scared to death of the putdowns and dismissals of those who didn't believe in SAHMs and wanting "talking points" to deal with the arguments thrown at them to dissuade them from raising their own children.

My first answer to these distraught women is to remind them that guilt often leads to defensiveness, which leads to hostility. The women who attack them know that the SAHMs are doing the right thing, and they aren't; that guilt leads them to deny the value of what they are not doing. Arguing with people who are defending themselves—rather than defending a philosophical point—is not going to be a clean, objective discussion at all. Therefore, don't bother arguing. Instead, simply come to that place inside yourself where you are at peace with your decision, and simply smile. That's it! Just smile.

You know that there are no worries about what your kids are being taught or how they're being treated, or how they're feeling, or what they're doing, because *you are there!*

You want to be the one to feed, hold, and love your baby. You want to be the one to experience every new synaptic brain connection that leads them to their next ability. You want to be the mother.

And please, realize that you don't have to be a perfect mother, or be perfect to be a mother. Being there—even when you're learning on the job—is the most important factor. No one is perfect at parenting, and the parameters change daily as your child transforms into an adult. It's all about the time, attention, love, compassion, direction, support, and hugs and kisses—and that's true no matter how old they are!

When you make the decision to *enjoy* being a SAHM, more important than the decision to simply be a SAHM, you'll discover all sorts of things about yourself. One woman wrote that she found out she has an infinite amount of patience that had never before been present in her life. "I can sit on the floor and play with a box of peanuts for forty-five minutes, and the time just flies. I can hold a crying baby for hours at night and never wish to be anywhere else in the world. I can withstand any tantrum . . . okay, maybe not any tantrum, but your average tantrum . . . with love."

Remember that distinction, please: enjoying versus just doing. "Enjoying" is sometimes a decision; at other times, it is a wonderful surprise.

BLOWING IT—BIG-TIME

I believe it is important not to "whitewash" the SAHM decision. Please let me warn you about an attitude issue I mentioned earlier in the book, because it needs repeating and more repeating. The value system of these times looks at SAHMs as a drain on the family finances, and an imposition on the husband who bears the weight of supporting the family. As women have been brainwashed by the feminista mentality, so have the men. Too many men, other than those with more conservative and religious upbringings, see a wife as a second opportunity for affording things and having status.

Many men even seem drawn to what appears glamorous and challenging in an independent career woman. Having fallen into this trap, sadly I think, these men then regret once they are married that they don't have a giving "mother earth" type wife to make the house a home and make her family a loving priority.

Nonetheless, this problem of societal values and how they have minimized "choice" and maximized "acquisition and self-centeredness" impacts both the SAHM and her husband. Many SAHMs end up in divorces; feeling so diminished by society, they end up, in their embarrassment and self-doubt, taking it out on those around them. One such divorced SAHM wrote, "Although I sought out the company of other SAHMs, we shared a collective sense of embarrassment. Why were we tripping over Lego pieces instead of using that valuable college degree? Why was the fridge adorned in plastic alphabet letters instead of memos on how to better the planet? To compensate for our imagined shortcomings, we busied ourselves with volunteer work and complaining. [Unfortunately], our complaints were usually directed at our husbands."

Whining loves company, and shared whining generally results in a magnification of negative feelings, which usually result in a lousier mood and less cordial behavior toward one's spouse. I generally recommend that women find other women who are more upbeat about life—even with its challenges and predicaments!

The divorced SAHM then went on to describe the irony of it all:

> *Instead of leaning back and enjoying the fruits of our collective labors, I now depend on a monthly spousal support check. Instead of anticipating graduations, weddings, and the birth of grandchildren together, we now correspond by e-mail when discussing matters relating to our grown children, and bear the awkward humiliation of sitting separately at ceremonies.*
>
> *All this could have been avoided, I believe, had I stood firmer for what I believed in. In the past years I have had plenty of time to pursue a career as a writer and editor, and I think that my life's experiences (forged during those cold winters, watching my cherubic babies transform themselves into thorny adolescents) have served me well.*

Let me remind you ladies that being a SAHM is not all about the kiddies; it is all about the family, and that includes a husband who needs your attention, affection, and approval as much as you need his. If you allow the condescending attitudes "out there" to seep into your home via your attitude, then the whole point of your efforts and sacrifice will be lost.

That means that when you get into the "My life is meaningless," "Poor me, I'm giving so much of myself and getting so little," or "Where is the *me* time?" complaints, you're surely in self-destruct mode. And when you self-destruct, the whole family goes down with you, because, accept it or not, the woman is the center of the universe, the very breath of a family.

Sure, it's understandable to have one of those feelings, but as I mentioned earlier, it's all about perspective. One such perspective:

I never realized how much children actually change every single day. My daughter is twenty months old, and it seems like she has a new word or cute little thing that she does each day. I have been there for all of her "firsts" so far, and you can't compare that to anything in the world.

The first time my daughter stretched out her little arms to me . . . I just about bawled my eyes out. One of my favorite things to do is to watch her playing without her knowing. She'll sit on the floor and play with her stuffed animals or "read" her books. It touches me in such a way that I never imagined I could feel. Seeing my daughter do something that I taught her is amazing to me. I really believe that moments like this can't be compared to anything else. To me, raising my child is what life is all about.

The key of perspective is that what you feel is put second to what you've *lived.* You can feel severely tired after a long day and gripe about the aches, pains, and pure exhaustion, or you can say to yourself, "You know, at the end of the day, it's kind of great to feel this worn out—it means I've experienced a lot today." Share the experiences as a blessing, instead of cursing the aches.

"It is important," as one SAHM wrote, "to shield your family from your personal sufferings from feeling small, bored, frustrated, stupid, tired, sick, mad, confused, and a whole lot of others. One has only to look at what one has . . . a wonderful, loving husband, children, a roof over our heads, food in the fridge, and a warm bed to cuddle in at night."

Those are wise words. That means you have to "stifle yourself." Well, in a word, yes! Venting every feeling isn't mature. Learning to deal with uncomfortable and unpleasant feelings is an important aspect of maturity. The pop-psych notion that you have to divulge every unpleasantness or you will have gangrene of the soul and spirit is ultimate nonsense. Learning to endure, transform by perspective or action, and be grateful is the fast lane to a good life. That's right. Having great luck and fortune is not the conduit to loving and enjoyable life; gratitude is.

GO WITH THE FLOW

One of the deadly traps of being a SAHM is the expectation that you can handle and control everything. Fuggedaboutit. If you get so caught up in trying to be on top of everything and in charge of everything and complete everything and be perfect at everything . . . you'll go nutty! You notice that in hurricane-level winds, it's the tree that gracefully bends that doesn't break. You have to become that graceful tree. Kids, husbands, dogs, electronic gizmos, refrigerators, bugs, and so forth can come at you in ways you'd never imagined and gang up on you when you least expect it. So, get used to thinking in triage form; that is, make a quick decision about priorities and stick with it without one ounce of self-doubt or second thoughts. Patience is not a virtue that people are born with; it's an ability one develops with practice. Deep breathing and dancing to the oldies in your kitchen will definitely be of service to you in this department.

And when you haven't shown patience, when you haven't gone with the flow—then what? Remember these five things:

1. Tomorrow is another day . . . thank goodness!

2. Most mistakes can be fixed . . . figure it out or ask for help.

3. It is never as bad as you think . . . not really.

4. A lot more good than lousy things happened today . . . admit it.

5. Everybody still loves you . . . let people hug you.

Read This and Tell Me You Still Don't Think You're Important

I stayed at home with my children. When my daughter was about two or three months old, I observed her looking at her hands. She had them close to her face and was exploring them as she moved them and touched them.

Her big brown eyes were wide, and her mouth was in the shape of an O. She was sitting in her little carrier while I was getting ready for the day. I got down to her level and smiled, and she put her hands up and showed them to me, her eyes bright like she was saying, "Look at these amazing things I have." I touched them and said, "There are your hands," and then I showed her my hands.

It was a sacred moment I will never forget. I know that if I had been a busy mom, trying to hurry and get ready and be somewhere, this moment never would have happened. Our home was serene. I wasn't rushed.

My daughter is now fifteen, and I still remember this experience we shared.

That is not the end of the story. When her daughter was in first grade, the child was diagnosed with dysgraphia, a condition in which the mind has a hard time telling the hands what to put on paper, and she struggled with writing during her elementary school years.

Obviously, the little girl would get very frustrated, as she was very intelligent but could not get her hands to do what she willed them to.

When she would get upset, I would grab her hands and remind her of the first time she discovered them and how precious they were to her. This would always calm her down, and she would try again. Now that she is in high school, she has overcome this disability and can write well. I'm so glad I had this experience when she was little in our calm home, where I had time to notice this little miracle.

I get furious when feministas proclaim quality time as more important that quantity time. What the heck are they thinking? Do they think you can plan quality time? Of course you can't! It happens here and there. Quality time needs quantity time to find a place to happen.

BEING A SAHM IS THE CURE!

A lot of women come from homes with extreme expectations and demands for perfection in order to be acceptable, to be accepted, or even to feel loved. Many women wrote me that the experience of becoming a SAHM was the cure. "Since childhood, I pressured myself to do more, more, more, and do it just so. I didn't realize the effect that stress had on me. We live in such a fast-paced world, but it is okay to slow down. I've learned to suppress my perfectionistic tendencies, and guess what? I'm a happier, healthier, more relaxed person. A calm mom makes a calm home and family."

The requirements of a good home have more to do with serenity, acceptance, love, and support than gold medals for the least amount of time in which the most tasks can be accomplished.

Another woman related her "SAHM cure" for a self-destructive lifestyle. She'd had a very successful and glamorous career in the fashion and home furnishings industry, traveling all over the world getting recognition and press. She'd developed a severe depression after her daughter was born, and spent three months on medications. She stopped the medication so that she could go back to work, thinking the meds would hamper her creativity.

She was back to traveling, with a nanny at home to take care of her child, and no one there to take care of her marriage. She and her husband went to a counselor, who simply asked the obvious question, "Why do you work?" Well, she thought she had to, to help with the bills; but it turned out that when they added it all up— nanny, travel expenses, wardrobe, commuting, and so on—she wasn't making much extra at all! She quit the next day.

Her whole family, especially her mother, gave her grief over taking this step. Everybody thought this was not going to be "good for her." She realized that they weren't considering her child, her husband, or her family at all.

This is the postfeminista generation. My mother worked and hardly paid any attention to us. In fact, my father was more like my mother. Anyway, surprise, surprise . . . I fell madly in love with being my child's mother. The opportunity to be a complete mother is the biggest gift from God I could imagine. This is the role for me. I was born to be their mother.

Yes, I have other strengths and capabilities. I am an artist and designer (which I now do success-fully from home while the children are in school), but the nurturing of my family is what completely fills my soul every single day.

SUMMARY THOUGHT

I know that for me, personally, being a SAHM was my cure. I grew up with a mother who had amazing talents (art and finance) but would never risk challenge—or potential failure—and in her frustration was quite neg-ative about motherhood, men, and marriage as well as unloving to her children and husband.

I grew up with a father who was ferociously self-critical and took it out on everyone around him. He was always telling me that I was stupid and lazy.

My response to all of this, as an innocent kid, was to try to please them all the time, and as an adult I would fly into rages when I couldn't be perfect at something. I had never known love from a parent, only criticism.

Consequently, I didn't want to get married or become a mother.

Finally, at thirty-five years of age, I realized that I was missing something from my life that being successful and taking on ever new challenges didn't fulfill. A chance viewing of a PBS *NOVA* program on conception to childbirth (in sixty minutes . . . yeah, right) ending with the newborn baby being put on Mommy's chest with Daddy cutting the umbilical cord—with everyone glowing—reached me, and that was the end of my feminista era.

Being a SAHM was fabulous—even though it was very difficult. It was my second chance to have a mother-child relationship. The first one was a bust. But this second one? Well, my son is in the military and says, "I love you, Mom," every time we end a phone conversation. And when he sees me on a visit, he picks me up off the ground and gives me a slurpy kiss, or turns me upside down and spins me—yipes!

I was there for every moment. It made me a better woman and a better person. I can't say that all the damage done by my original family doesn't still haunt me; it does. But my life would have been bereft of deeper meaning and experiences without marriage and motherhood.

7

THE GOOD, THE BAD, THE UNFORGETTABLE

There are good, bad, and unforgettable qualities to every experience we have. Here's an example, as it relates to exercise in my life.

THE GOOD

I work out with a trainer three times each week, and with a yoga instructor twice each week to stretch out what the workout has tightened up. I also hike up mountains, race sailboats, ride a motorcycle, and shoot pool (hey, leaning over that table works your back and hips!). All this activity has toned up my body to an amazing degree. My "core" is like steel, and my balance is amazing—and I look fabulous in tight jeans!

THE BAD

That all sounds great, right? Well, it is. But that doesn't mean that it doesn't come with some negatives: waking up early every day to do the workouts, the strain and stress of doing the exercises, the annoying injuries that are a natural part of using your body hard, the relentless requirement to "keep it up" even during vacations and lazy days (you lose what you don't use), and the fees of the teachers (albeit well deserved) who make sure I keep up the schedule and do things properly to maximize results and minimize damage.

THE UNFORGETTABLE

The best part of the entire issue is that at sixty-one years of age, I am seemingly without limits (although I did chicken out when given the opportunity to land a jet fighter on a carrier!) for physical activity, and have such well developed muscles everywhere on my tiny body that I can avoid serious damage in everyday mishaps and readily endure hours of steering a sailboat through high winds and churning seas to have the kind of experiences that enrich a life. Oh, yeah, and I get a lot of whistles from hard hats—which I accept graciously!

The good, the bad, and the unforgettable are inherent qualities of any endeavor, and that includes being a SAHM. It is notable that "good" and "unforgettable" are two-thirds of the equation. And the one-third that is "bad"—well, some things can be improved, other things must be endured.

Some SAHMs have to deal with desperately ill or handicapped children. Some of these moms look at these situations as very, very bad and an unhappy burden—and no one can really argue with the sadness inherent in such a situation. Other moms have written to me saying such things as, "God knew what mother and family to send this child to for a quality life when He sent him to us."

In the more than thirty years I've been on radio talking to people, I've heard what seems like every possible side of every possible situation that could occur—and then I still get moved or surprised or disappointed in a unique way. But the unforgettable part of my career has been feeling like I've touched the divine, through some remarkable people who face life's challenges with a philosophical approach, a sense of humor, a feeling of gratitude for what they did have—and still have, in the people who love them, and a graciousness that allows, without bitterness, others to go on enjoying life.

In life, everything—everything—has good and bad elements. The most important lesson I'm still trying to learn myself, is that the "bad" should never be the end of the story, nor the decision maker—not when there also exist the "good" and the "unforgettable."

This is all by way of introduction to this chapter, which will deal with what SAHMs have found to be good, bad, and unforgettable in the experience of giving birth and raising a human being to be a decent, loving, contributing member of the world. The bad is real, and has to be dealt with, accepted, improved, and/or endured. The good needs no analysis—right? Wrong! The good must be emphasized and embraced with every breath you take, or you might be overrun by the lousy feelings from the bad. The unforgettable is . . . well . . . unforgettable. And for those moments, you probably need tissues if you're wearing a short-sleeved shirt.

"THE GOOD"—THE HIGH POINTS

The mother of a nineteen-year-old daughter forwarded to me, with great pride, a letter to the editor that her daughter wrote to the *Edmonton* (Alberta, Canada) *Sun* in response to an article she had read, written by a woman who was talking about how women today are wanting "full lives, which is almost impossible to achieve with a house full of kids." She said, "My daughter was very disheartened and decided to respond herself with the following letter. Needless to say, I am this day once again proud to be my kid's mom, and I thought you would appreciate it too."

Here's the letter from Kate Walsh:

> I was saddened to read Ms. Jacobs' column in Wednesday's paper, entitled, "Parenthood Now a Pricey Optional Extra." Although she quoted a good number of statistics (and we all know that statistics don't lie), I wasn't sure where she stood on the matter until the second-to-last paragraph, where she stated that "women want full lives, and that's almost impossible to achieve with a house full of kids."
>
> Granted, she did use the word "almost," however I can't help but wonder why anyone would think that raising children in and of itself does not constitute a "full life." I can't think of anything more rewarding than taking part in such a miracle as the creation of life, and then to have the privilege of raising those miracles from babyhood to adulthood and having them call you "mom." To me, that seems like the most "full" option available to me as a young woman.

I was moved to read such sentiments from a teen-ager, especially during these "progressive" times of mothering-by-proxy. It would seem the first "good" is simply *feeling* the miracle and the privilege. Stop for a moment, whether or not you are a mom yet, and just close your eyes and imagine the miracle of creation—in love and passion creating a new life. Then—now keep your eyes closed . . . hmmm, after reading this paragraph, of course—and think about the awesome opportunity you have to mold a person, teaching right from wrong, motivating charity and compassion, play-ing together, enjoying those sweet, affectionate or silly moments, watching your child strive and succeed, and getting and giving hugs.

One of my fondest memories was when Deryk was able to finally sit up without falling over . . . often. We were rolling a ball back and forth between us as we sat spread-legged on the floor. I guess my rolling needed work, because the ball rolled slightly under the chair off to his left. He looked at me, then at the ball, repeating the cycle a few times, and then began to whimper with a bit of confusion and frustration. I pointed to the ball and kept urging him to try to get it himself. Finally, he worked himself over to the chair, reached under, gripped the ball, and dragged it out to great shouts of celebratory approval from his mommy. I'll never forget the look on his face—pure joy.

I felt like I was a part of something serious and wonderful: in those moments, I helped him strive for something seemingly beyond his reach; trusting me, he went for it and conquered an important task and life lesson—all because I was *there* to roll a ball.

Hugs and kisses are necessary, but not sufficient; support, inspiration, motivation, and enthusiasm for developmental successes are essential. How wonderful it is to be there to participate in these great moments!

Furthermore, as one SAHM wrote,

> *High points have been going to the parks on beautiful days with my kids, while others are slaving away in their offices; having a relaxing morning with my kids; not having to worry about a job when my kids are sick; being home to greet my husband at the end of his workday; making our house an actual home; and most of all, not having double duty of work and the care of children and home.*
>
> *Lately it's been fun to watch people treat me as if I am uneducated, since I stay home, but I know just how intelligent I am and how much my family appreciates me.*

This SAHM brings up a point that appears to be consistent with the sentiment of most SAHMs—that is, the ability to focus solely on family. One SAHM described it well as she talked about her experience as a "working for pay" mother; she was so burdened with all the disparate responsibilities that she actually had no focus, not on her husband, her marriage, her daughter, her household—or, frankly, even her career. Many such moms complain that no matter where they are and what they're doing, they are thinking of where they're not.

As one SAHM put it, "Now, despite what I've heard other feminist types say, I DO have it all as a SAHM. I'm doing it all better than I did when I also worked outside the home. I can't describe the enormous satisfaction in that. Staying at home full-time is certainly not all roses, but the worst day at home with my husband and kids is by far better than attempting to 'balance' it all and in the process letting everything suffer."

It would seem that simplification brings increased peace and satisfaction and decreased chaos and frustration. That's definitely a good thing.

It would seem that the greatest joy of "being there" is *being there*. Being there to play, share, teach, and enjoy the everyday activities that were taken for granted before seen through the eyes of children.

And boy oh boy, kids do see things. For example, one mother wrote that her eight-year-old daughter takes lunch to school because they are on a budget; a budget the little girl does not know about. All the child knows is that every day she gets a sandwich cut with various cookie cutters (hearts, animals, etc.) with a cutesy note from Mommy. If Mom were working, she'd most likely be rushing out the door and have no time for such personal lunch making. This little girl's friends see what her mom does and are quite jealous of this extra attention.

Parents always call me, wanting to know how to discipline their children to teach patience and postponement of gratification—two biggies! One mother's everyday routine with her four-year-old son produces this education without pain. Her son asked her one day after breakfast if they could go to the park to play Frisbee. She said they could, but right after the breakfast dishes were put away. He helped put his dish in the sink and went to brush his teeth without Mom nagging—all to get ready to go to the park. Most parents want to know how to teach their children this, because they are not in an environment where they can learn it naturally.

One SAHM listed her "highs":

- Seeing all the "firsts"—steps, words, smiles.

- Having a friend say, "Your kids are so well-behaved," and knowing that was because I was with them and not at work.

- When my husband told me that I was "contributing to the greater good of society by staying home and raising our two boys." That was the best "raise" I ever got!

"THE BAD"—THE LOW POINTS

While some SAHMs humorously declare that all they've missed by being at home with and for their family is pressure, guilt, and an early heart attack, there *are* some stresses and strains involved in this situation.

One obvious "bad" is the concern that once a career or professional woman gets off the train, it will be difficult to get a ticket later on, once the children are all in school or out of the home as adults. This is a reasonable concern. When women call me, disquieted about this problem, I tell them the following:

- You may not even want to go back—time will tell.

- Sometimes it's difficult to perceive what options will be available at different times of history and your life.

- All of life is a trade-off, and something's gotta give in order for you to get something else of value.

- Your growing maturity, wisdom, and experiences might lead you into some new adventure in the future that you've never even thought about or considered.

The truth is, there are no guarantees in life, whether or not you're a SAHM. Certainly world and domestic politics and economics have an impact on everybody's plans. Nobody can even be sure that the jobs they're continuing in will not become obsolete. The best way to handle life is not to agitate over what might be, but to enjoy what is and endeavor to be flexible and creative enough to take on life as it unpredictably rolls along.

Some SAHMs have periods when they miss their work, and that's perfectly natural—even expected! First of all, don't assume that feeling is an omen that you've made the wrong choice. Missing your long hair once you've bobbed it doesn't mean you shouldn't have cut it; most likely it just means that there are some aspects not available to you—like a ponytail when you're having a bad-hair day. So instead of feeling sorry for yourself, realize that your life, just like a developing child's, has phases—and now you're in the mommy phase.

And don't forget that you're glamorizing the work situation because you're having a lull in energy and daily joy. After all, there are plenty of things we don't like about work: remember the politics and gossiping? Remember the commute? Remember the relentless deadlines and irritations? Remember how tired you were when you got home? Perhaps you were too tired to enjoy the fruits of your labors.

When you got fed up at work, you couldn't up and leave for a break. As a SAHM, you can pick up the kiddies and go and do anything you darn well please. Enjoy that flexibility instead of getting mucked up in the annoyance you're feeling at your routine of child and home care.

Second, this is the time to reboot! Take your kids and go to the beach to build sand castles or romp in the ocean. Take your kids and go to the local kids' museum or zoo and point and oooh and ahhh at all the wonders—especially the spiders, if you have sons. You could simply go to the park and watch your kids play and chase butterflies. Just hanging around the house is deadly—get out and experience the world together; do things you've never done before!

Third, pick yourself up and bring your kids to the homes of other SAHMs for girl talk, support, activities, charitable and community efforts, or just hanging out for a while.

Some moms take their restlessness and turn it into creativity that doesn't compromise their families—and even adds to them, contributing extra income and, frankly, a better attitude. For those of you who can switch gears well, take inspiration from one SAHM, who wrote that, feeling adrift in laundry and runny noses, she was bored and longed for excitement. "Shortly thereafter I found a new hobby and actually opened a business that I ran while the kids were asleep. I was able to still be home with them and focus on them as well as have a creative outlet for some of my pent-up energy."

I remember talking to one hostile women's group about such endeavors and receiving nary a smile or nod, much less applause. However, months later one of the mothers in attendance found me at another event and told me that she had started to bake muffins and, with her baby with her, went around to the adjacent office buildings and sold them for lunch and snacks to employees of the various companies. She felt wonderful that she had a creative outlet and never had to compromise time with her infant, since the baking was at home, and the delivery time—with baby—wasn't long.

For some moms, the low point of staying at home is the repetitive nature of housework and the relentless needs of children—creatures whose actions and attitudes cannot be easily controlled. My answer to these mothers is, "Give it up, woman! Trying to have everything in order all the time is a ridiculous expectation to have for yourself! Give yourself a break!" I remember one woman coming to my home when Deryk was about four and sneering at our "living room," which was really a giant toy box and playground. I almost felt embarrassed—almost—and then said, "I like to spend my time having a grand ol' time with my son. There will be plenty of time in my future when my living room will look more traditional—until, of course, I have grandchildren!"

Now, there have been calls from men complaining that they work hard all day to provide so that their wives can stay home with the children, and they don't like coming home to a messy place. There are two issues here. The first is that these men need more compliments and appreciation for their efforts—kisses, hugs, and words of adoration work just fine. If they don't get this supportive feedback, they tend to see the messy house as a demonstration that they aren't cared about. The second issue is that some men are indeed a bit compulsive, and lack of order is distressing to them. I ask these men, "Would you rather come home to a perfect house, or come home to peace, happiness, joy, enthusiasm, and love? Sir, there isn't enough time to do and have both. You get to pick." They generally want the love stuff; and when they are too unnerved to make that selection, I help them get to the core of their childhood's absence of affection, replaced by order. It generally helps them.

Many women have had the same upbringing and equate order with being lovable. Please, please disconnect those two. There never is perfect order; does that mean that you'll never be lovable enough? Does that sound like a good plan for a quality life? I hope you said, "Nope."

Finances are generally a low point—living on one salary is a challenge. You can mope about it and beat your husband up nightly over it, or you can learn to be creative. Many SAHMs come up with clever ideas, teaming up with friends with coupon exchanges, buying in bulk, sharing children's clothes and toys, planning camping vacations, and budgeting efficiently. You'll find other ideas in the appendix, "Dr. Laura's Resources for Stay-at-Home Moms," at the end of this book.

I remember when my father talked about wishing we could afford to put a little patio in our backyard, extending from the back sliding doors. My mother, without saying a word, went upstairs for about two minutes, and when she came down, she had a roll of money to hand to my dad. Astounded, he asked where she got the money from. She had managed to put a little away each week by not wasting money. You'd never have known, because we always had food on the table, and the house always looked pretty. Several weeks later, we had a nice little patio.

You can look down on your circumstances, or you can take on the challenge and do something with it that will make you proud, and the family hero! You can make your life fun and exciting by taking the viewpoint that a disadvantage is an opportunity, or you can dismiss the value of family for a shallow notion of what success really is. You know which side of this I'm on.

Another low point is the attitude many working mothers (WMs) have about your time and availability to take on *their* responsibilities. Too many of these WMs think your time is not as valuable as theirs, and take advantage of you by asking you to pick up their kids from school or activities, babysit their infants and children during the day or evening for no or little financial compensation, run errands, and just generally be accommodating to their schedules. You need to learn to say, "I'm sorry, I would really like to help you, but I've got so much to do for my family, and I really don't feel right taking time away from my children and husband."

The only way you are going to get respect from others is by demonstrating your own respect for what you are doing. What better way to do that than to explain how needed you are, and where your responsibilities are? And it gives detractors a message that they've been avoiding: family comes first.

While family should come first, you do need some time to decompress. It's good to work a plan out with your husband (or your mother or mother-in-law) to give you some time when you can take a bath or a walk, nap, exercise, write letters, get your hair done, have a manicure, whatever, so that you, just like a computer, can reboot your energies and enthusiasm. It's okay to ask for help. SAHM may start with an *S*, but it does not mean superwoman. You're human, and a break is necessary—or you will break.

It is important to try to pace yourself during the day. Nap when the kids nap; make sure you have nutritious snacks and meals that keep your energy and your health up; find ways to have your children help with the chores, so they become fun rather than tedious burdens; reward yourself in thought, word, and deed; and plan to use your husband as a loving, sexual release at the end of a long day.

Take girl-time breaks. Guys get together with their buddies and spend a weekend fishing, drinking beer, playing poker, camping, and being weekend sports warriors. Women have to dump the guilt portion of their psyches and sign up for the female version. Yes, you'll miss your kids; yes, no one in the world can be the mommy you can; yes, you'll be missed by a husband who won't do everything exactly the way you would, though his way is good too. But everyone needs to decompress, and SAHMs are high on that list. So—get your girlfriends together a couple of times a year and have a good time, girl-style.

Another low point is when you realize that a child who is willful, stubborn, challenging, or extremely energetic is not exactly what you had in mind when you said to yourself, "I want to have a baby." This is when your mother, aunts, and grandmothers come in very handy; they've been there, done that. Their advice should be sought after, not taken as some kind of message that you're incompetent as a mother. When you find yourself getting into nose-to-nose battles with a toddler, you know it's time to get some help. There are books to assist you, and SAHMs' Web sites where you can share experiences, ask questions, and get advice and support (see the appendix, "Dr. Laura's Resources for Stay-at-Home Moms").

The important thing is, never be afraid to admit you're having some trouble. That will just make it worse for you and the whole family. Every parent has had self-doubts and problems dealing with kids. It is the human experience. Tap into the resources available as soon as you can without beating yourself up.

Sometimes all of this will just drive you crazy. Everyone has a bad day or week. And remember, that is true whether you are at work or at home. The benefit of a SAHM is that it is also warm and mushy being a loving mommy and wife.

One SAHM forwarded this adorable e-mail to me, which sums up mommyhood beautifully:

Dear Santa:

I've been a good mom all year. I've fed, cleaned and cuddled my children on demand, visited the doctor's office more than my doctor and sold 62 cases of candy bars to raise money to plant a shade tree on the school playground. I was hoping you could spread my Christmas list over several years, since I had to write this letter with my son's red crayon on the back of a receipt in the laundry room between cycles, and who knows if I'll find any more free time in the next 18 years.

Here are my wishes: I'd like a pair of legs that don't ache (in any color except purple, which I already have) and arms that don't hurt or flap in the breeze, but are strong enough to pull my screaming child out of the candy aisle in the grocery store.

I'd also like a waist, since I lost mine somewhere in the 7th month of my last pregnancy. If you're hauling big-ticket items this year, I'd like fingerprint-resistant windows and a radio that only plays adult music, and a refrigerator with a secret compartment behind the crisper where I can hide to talk on the phone.

On the practical side, I could use a talking doll that says, "Yes, Mommy," to boost my parental confidence, along with two kids who don't fight and three jean skirts that will zip all the way up without the use of power tools.

I could also use a recording of Tibetan monks chanting "Don't eat in the living room" and "Take your hands off your sister," because my voice seems to be just out of my children's hearing range and can only be heard by the dog.

If it's too late to find any of these products, I'd settle for enough time to brush my teeth and comb my hair in the same morning, or the luxury of eating food warmer than room temperature without it being served in a Styrofoam container.

If you don't mind, I could also use a few miracles to brighten the holiday season. Would it be too *much trouble to declare ketchup a vegetable? It will clear my conscience immensely. It would also be helpful if you could coerce my children to help around the house without demanding payment as if they were the bosses of an organized crime family.*

Well, Santa, the buzzer on the dryer is calling my name, and my son saw my feet under the laundry room door. I think he wants his crayon back.

Yours always, Mom.

P.S.: One more thing . . . you can cancel all my requests if you can keep my children young enough to always believe in Santa.

Awwwwww.

THE UNFORGETTABLE

Recently, a caller complained to me that she was tired of the everyday tasks of being a mom. I asked her about her day, and it became clear by her answer that she was spending all of her time being a devoted housekeeper, not a SAHM. I asked her if her child were home. When she answered in the affirmative, I told her to take the cordless phone with her to her daughter's room, put it down without hanging up, and simply tickle her daughter. Somewhat stunned at my odd request, she followed my request.

On the air was the sound of feet padding off down the hall, a door opening, a child's voice wondering what Mom wanted, silence, and then tons of giggles from Mom and child. When the mom got back on the phone, I said, while she sniffed tears, "That's why you're home."

I received a ton of mail demonstrating a huge positive reaction to that call. This one was particularly gratifying:

> That day (of the call) I was feeling frustrated that my two-year-old daughter got into my designer purse, took my liquid foundation and smeared it all over my hardwood floor, expensive purse, walls, her hair and face. The call touched me because as I look back at how upset I was . . . I turned my frustration into gratefulness that I have a healthy, fun daughter to be able to stay home with, love, and really be present in her life.

> When you asked the caller, who was complaining so bitterly about her child, how her life might be better if her child were gone, and suggesting she would be empty . . . that hit a nerve with me because smearing foundation all over everything is actually pretty funny.

I have been a listener of yours since I was seventeen. I didn't have good role models in my life. I am now thirty-one with three kids and a husband that I take care of and don't take for granted. I think listening to you for all these years has helped prepare me to be a great wife and mom.

Another caller complained that she wasn't feeling fulfilled because she wasn't doing enough. My response to her evidently also touched a few hearts and psyches:

I have been feeling the same way, and it dawned on me that I need to focus on making my house a home. I have three children, ages two and under, so I am often overwhelmed.

Well, I took your advice today, blasted some fun music that also appeals to my kids (they like musicals too) and we cleaned up the kitchen, family room and dining room in record time. My twin nine-month-olds loved watching Mom dance around the house, cleaning and singing to them. And my two-year-old pranced around with me, with a brush in hand, singing along.

We had so much fun, bonding together and getting our HOME ready for when Dad arrived. He stopped at the door and asked, "Where am I?" We had a great dinner and lovely evening together as a family. Thank you for all your support of SAHMs everywhere. I love being my kids' mom and husband's wife and I DO get fulfillment when I focus on being just that. Thanks!

One of my favorite letters was from a SAHM of three boys, nine, five, and two. She admitted to being overwhelmed and feeling sorry for herself. This particular morning she was waiting to sign her five-year-old to a two-day-a-week morning Christian preschool. Noticing almost all the other mothers in great shoes, hip clothing, gorgeous hair highlights, and manicures brought up feelings of envy, and embarrassment and shame for how she looked in her long dishwater-blond ponytail and frumpy ten-year-old maternity top for her fourth pregnancy.

Suddenly, she realized she was feeling sorry for the wrong people.

Where I will be back in two and a half hours to pick up my son, the local day-care owner will be here to pick up her daughter along with several other children. Where her daughter will be lined up and herded to the waiting day-care car, I'll be holding my son's hand while he excitedly tells me about his lesson and what he had for a snack. I'll stop by the park and push the boys on the swings before heading home for PB&J sandwiches. Her daughter will be warehoused for the next five to seven hours until her stressed, yet fashionable mother picks her up.

So as I sat this morning snuggling with my sleepy two-year-old, these lines, inspired by that popular TV commercial, popped into my head, and I would like to share them with you. Thank you for helping me keep grounded and focused on what matters.

- High-fashion shoes and business suit: $325

- Cut, highlights, and manicure: $160

- Fifty hours of day care a week: $400

- *Skipping it all to snuggle on the couch in PJs with your little ones: Priceless*

Living the simple life to be home raising your babies is priceless . . . for everything else there is a credit card debit!

SUMMARY THOUGHT

This afternoon as I was driving my eight-year-old son home from school," wrote a SAHM, he asked if he could have a play date with one of his neighborhood friends. I reminded him that this particular boy has to go to a child day-care center (CDC) before and after school because his mom and dad both work.

My son then proceeded to tell me that he's glad that I don't work because at the CDC you don't get to do whatever you want, like go to the fridge to get a snack or go to your room to play with your toys, which he enjoys immensely after a long, structured day at school. He continued with, "Mom, do you know why I like to be in the kitchen so much?" I replied that I didn't and could he please tell me. My adorable son then went on to tell me that it's because I'm there.

At this point, I considered stopping the car, swooping him up, and smooching him all over his cute little face; but since we were so close to home, I waited and did so as soon as we were safely in the driveway. His innocent little comment brought tears to my eyes, joy to my heart, and reminded me that as hard as parenting can sometimes be, the rewards are priceless.

8

GREAT ADVICE

Sometimes the last thing we all want is great advice. Why the last? It's not unusual to be afraid or uncomfortable asking for advice; we all have some degree of trouble admitting we don't know something, or that we have fears or limitations, or that we're making mistakes.

I remember those first few months, after a traumatic C-section, and with a child who seemed to never stop crying (I kept wondering, Where's the "cute" part?), when I called one of my girlfriends who already had a child, desperately needing some support but ashamed to admit that I wasn't feeling all maternally loving all the time. I was exhausted, frustrated, and confused as to why Deryk was crying when I was being so, well, "motherly" (huggy, kissy, etc.). I timidly beat around the bush, finally hinting at how difficult it all seemed, when she said with a boisterous laugh, "Oh, my, Laura, I've had so many times when I've wanted to toss the kid in the garbage compactor. That's just natural—don't worry about it, and it doesn't make you a bad mother to feel that way." We both laughed.

Whew! Did I ever feel relieved to hear from another mother who was equally frustrated at times that not feeling happy about it all the time was, well, normal! That took my anxiety level all the way down to just about zero. I no longer felt like a "bad mother" because in spite of my emotional difficulties, I was still behaving as though I was feeling all the good stuff. Getting validation that my unpleasant feelings were normal went a long way to help me relax into—ironically—feeling happier about the situation . . . even though it was still difficult.

Mothering behavior comes more naturally to just about every other mammal than to the human. For other animals, mothering is instinctual, meaning that the behavior is hardwired into their brains, not a matter of choice. While human beings are exceptional in having evolved brains that can reason and learn, we also have the ability to make bad, selfish, and destructive or good, gracious, and constructive decisions; we can make choices, and we have the ability to change, grow, and learn.

Advice is information—although a lot of advice is an expression of personal preference or experience, and not necessarily a guide that can be generalized to each child or mother's temperament. I've found that the best advice is simply support, so that Mommy can calm down, get off her own back, use her own creativity, and incorporate new information when and if it "feels right." Of course, there are some facts that mothers need to learn about what any child needs, and some tried-and-true tricks to help a child get calm, for example.

I remember getting tons of advice about how to get Deryk to stop crying long enough to nap: driving in the car, sitting in a baby swing or the rocking chair, jiggling his butt in the crib, and so forth. None of these seemed to work at all. I discovered that putting him in a stroller and pushing it over bumpy ground was the charm; this worked great to make him nap, but meant my "break" required hiking. Oh, well . . . at least I got a break from the crying, which made me feel so bad for him (assuming crying meant discomfort) as well as for myself (as I felt horrible that I couldn't just lay on mother hands and bring him peace).

While advice comes in all flavors and degrees of usefulness, it is a wise woman who taps into the experience of the women who come before. Just be careful not to "over" take advice from advice bullies, those women (even mothers and siblings) who will make you feel bad about yourself if you don't do exactly what they tell you to do. They'll just make you feel useless as a mother, and keep you from getting a feel for your child through trial and error.

My biggest piece of advice for you is this: if you're so wrapped up in the details that you can't relax and enjoy your child—you're on the wrong track! It is a far, far better thing you do to form a comfortable, loving bond than have all the latest gizmos, toys, or pop-psych techniques. The single reason *you* need to be there is to convey security, warmth, creature comforts, and love, love, love, love . . . because you can hire someone to feed one end and mop up the other, but only you are mommy love.

And let me remind you that the feeding/mopping up is part of the wonderful experience of mothering. I remember that before Deryk was born, and I still had some feminista remnants hanging off my psyche, I made it very clear to my husband that we would share all responsibilities for Deryk fifty-fifty—and that most definitely included diapering. However, what I discovered, to my absolute joy and amazement, was how much fun it was to change diapers: the giggles and wiggles turned out to be a surprise! I used to sneak and change his diapers all the time (no more fifty-fifty for me!) so that I could enjoy those moments. I have photos of the process that document the sheer loveliness of even changing dirty diapers. Also—I have threatened my son with showing these to his future wife, should he ever get on my wrong side!

The feeding issue actually comes in the same wrapper. Playing airplane and airplane hangar to get food into his mouth was frustrating at times, but an entertaining and challenging game. I couldn't understand how any kid could actually like pickles or cauliflower, or hold baby food in his mouth seemingly forever, and then strain it back out through several teeth and lips.

So don't, if at all possible, give up the "maintenance" exercises to anyone else—except, of course, to Daddy or a grandparent—because it makes vivid memories for you, and emotional memories for your child, which become the foundation for intuitive bonding.

What follows is the advice of SAHMs to help you feel more confident, competent, and happy with your choice. Perhaps this chapter should be renamed "Great Suggestions," as I don't want you to measure yourself by them and end up feeling bad about your style or ideas. We're just sharing here—experiment and synthesize your own style. Your way of dealing with your child will have lots of unique aspects, because you and your child are unique human beings, and the blend is yet another special level of uniqueness.

FIRST OF ALL

First of all, never argue about the "rightness" of staying home with your child(ren) with those who would say you are actually hurting them or keeping them from the kind of experiences they need. Just think to yourself, "How could mother love and attention be inferior or equal to institutionalized settings or hired help?"— and then smile and perhaps offer, "Maybe you're right, but I'm selfish enough to want to experience my child's life's adventures with him."

If you use the word *selfish*, it definitely makes it harder for people to argue with you: cute trick. Never duel with statistics, studies, reports, morning television talking heads selling books on relieving the guilt of full-time working women with children—just shrug and repeat the "selfish" sentence until they back off. In fact, start relating some lovely or funny story about something you and your child experienced, and then ask, "What has your day-care worker told you anytime this week that might be similar?" That will definitely back detractors off.

Also—compete neither in your mind or in your heart. Don't envy. Don't spend one precious moment yearning for cars, jewelry, vacations, furniture, or the size of a backyard. As the commercial says, "Some things are priceless." Whenever you are having a bit o' an envy attack, it's definitely time to hug and kiss a kid or a husband . . . yours, of course! As one SAHM proclaimed:

> I recommend a woman prepare for being a SAHM by strengthening her convictions to do so. This will give her the fortitude to ignore any negativity she may get (or feel) as a result of her decision. I really didn't get much negative reaction to my decision, and I think part of that was that people could tell I was completely sure of my decision, and there wasn't any point in challenging me. I never justify my decision to anyone, and I am not embarrassed when people ask me what I do and I say that I stay home with my kids.
>
> I used to have a senior position in an organization, and my work was highly respected. However, I have no need for anyone else's accolades anymore. . . . I get all the reinforcement I need every day seeing how well adjusted my children are and how much they appreciate me being home.

SECOND OF ALL

Remember that you are taking on a "traditional" role in the family; one which is considered by some to be outdated and a step backward for a woman. That is going to take some moxie on your part to accept, unless your background has prepared you for this. While it is called SAHM, the job requirements are much more far-ranging: cooking, housekeeping, managing the home expenses, paying bills, coordinating home repairs, and so forth.

One mistake many SAHMs can make, especially if they aren't completely sanguine about the entire job description, is to complain about their lot and to nag their husbands—both usually the moment he comes home from his job and commute. I have tried explaining to many a SAHM that this is division of labor: the home front is hers, and the dragon lair is his.

It is remarkable, however, that a husband who is shown appreciation and gets great lovin' is more than happy to pitch in with household chores.

Never, never, never consider any household chore more important than heaping warmies upon your family. Only you can turn a potentially loving experience into a work farm with a compulsive attitude about what has to be done, how, when, and by whom.

As one SAHM put it, "You have to clean the house, make dinner, and basically take care of all the household stuff, not just the kids. This is not a step backward for women; this is you making the choice to put your husband and kids first. It truly is a step forward. Also, prepare for the mundane. If you get caught up in how boring it can be, you will be miserable. Make it fun, and if you can't do it all . . . DON'T."

HAVE BREAK TIMES

Make sure that even with all that must be done to take care of home and family, you find time for a daily break. Sometimes that will mean you have to get up very early (I used to get up at 5:00 AM each day to have some time for myself to catch up with . . . whatever, or take a brisk walk or read the paper over a cup of hot tea), or use children's nap and/or school time to indulge yourself some way.

If you like outdoor activities, you can arrange to bike, run, or walk with the kids. This will jump-start your endorphins, keep you fit, and remove you from the in-a-rut feeling that sometimes goes hand in hand with housework and child care.

Trade off watching children with your close SAHM friends or the grandparents so that you can do some errands or get your hair and nails done (no reason to adopt the bag-lady look!). A couple of hours here and there can make all the difference in your attitude and perspective. Watch out that you don't get so compulsive that you make being a SAHM look like a different form of workaholic. If you don't make even a modest effort to take care of yourself, you risk burnout, depression, and becoming very bitchy (smile).

Being a SAHM doesn't mean you don't deserve or need a break. That's unrealistic. Everyone needs to recharge, and your child benefits tremendously from forming close relationships with other family members . . . without you hovering over them. You will find that with breaks, you will come back to your child, home, and husband with newfound enthusiasm and energy.

A SAHM suggests,

Find some other SAHMs. Get together with them even if it's just shopping together for groceries, exercising, or watching DVDs. Just get together at least once a week, at the same time, so that you don't have to think about going, you just go.

Take a nap when your kids take a nap, or just relax. Read a book while the laundry is going and the kid(s) are taking a nap. Take a bath or shower.

Remember to have some time for yourself to unwind, even if it is only fifteen minutes. ALWAYS treat your husband right. If you've been stressed out and you treat him right he will pay you back and take the kids off your back so that you can spend some time and relax.

Always find ways to get out of the house, especially in the winter. Go to a library and read books there. Go to a dinosaur museum, or any museum. Take your baby in a stroller around the track at your local recreation facility.

But most important of all, just have fun with your husband, your kid(s), and yourself. Humor is how we all make it through life.

BUDGET AND DEBT

One of the best things you can do to prepare for being a SAHM is eliminating all debt. The last thing you need is daily worry about bills and creditors. Spend a couple of years living off one salary and putting the second into savings and safe investments. This will make living on one salary more of an everyday way of life. When something becomes more familiar, it automatically becomes more comfortable and easier to do.

Budgeting might mean going for smaller and more fuel-efficient cars, a home in a family-friendly neighborhood (that might mean planning a move), and simply not spending on things that are not truly necessary, like a flat-screen TV in every room, including the bathroom.

One SAHM mused, "To prepare to be a SAHM, make sure you want to give it all for your child. Nothing is more important than that baby. If you need money in your pocket to buy that latte, or go shopping for new clothes all the time, or go out to eat every other night, get eight-plus hours of sleep, or a manicure/pedicure every week, then being a SAHM may not be for you. [Otherwise] do it—your children will thank you every day."

Get organized. On and off the Internet, look for sales and coupon clubs. Organize recipes that you can make for cheap. Clip coupons from your local newspaper and from the junk mail that comes to your home. Your new "job" is basically going to be figuring out how to best use the resources you have. There is a great sense of accomplishment and satisfaction in squeezing blood out of a stone. Impress the heck out of yourself and your family by making the home beautiful and the dinner scrumptious. Make mealtimes comforting and memorable. Remember—for yourself, your husband, and your children, the whole point is to enjoy the day and build memories.

THE "RIGHT" HUSBAND

I have often said that the key to the perfect marriage is, "Choose wisely, and treat kindly." The support of your husband is crucial. It is so important that from the very beginning your husband be comfortable with the idea—no, more than comfortable, actually enthusiastic about being responsible for providing and protecting while you are nurturing and creating the entire attitude and environment of a home, not just a house. The last thing you need is a man-boy who pouts about not having more money to buy more things, and whines about how much pressure this gives him.

As one SAHM wrote, "This means that when they are asked at the office/job, 'What does your wife do?' they can answer with a sense of pride, 'She takes care of our world.'"

So, hopefully you've married a real man who not only takes pride in what you do for the family every day, but sees providing not as a stressful burden but as a blessed opportunity.

If you haven't married such a man, and you yearn to be a SAHM, it's going to take, as I've said earlier in this book, a lot of conversation, with you not arguing, demanding, or insulting; instead, you need to show your man how important it is to you, a child, and him that you will be doing (name all the things), and that you look forward to being so deeply appreciative of his "dragon slaying" for the family. In fact, tell him it'll up your respect for him as well as the sexiness of his image. Women do tend to look up with more respect, admiration, and appreciation to the men who "take care of them" than to those who lead unisex lives with them. And I believe the reverse is also true: men have more affection and regard for women who make them feel important and like "heroes."

INCORPORATING PART-TIME WORK/ACTIVITIES

One SAHM wrote to tell me that she suggests women be prepared when they're young for the lifestyle they most value. "Know what you want and don't compromise—you can only do what you plan for, and then you have to make it work."

She planned her future life when she was eighteen years old. She started a dance business with the idea that someday she could work just a little and make good money with a skill. Currently, as a SAHM, she works six hours a week, teaching at night. She makes some extra money, and her kids have her home every day. Her five-year-old goes with her and dances.

"I have the best life," she wrote; "I am teaching the young women that I work with the tips of finding something they love and making it a business so they can enjoy their own children someday."

In this young woman's case, she had a skill that was a love—dancing—and she worked it around her family, not the other way around.

I used to take care of Deryk all day and then go to work at a radio station at 9:00 PM, after his bedtime. Was I tired? Yes! Was I satisfied? I got to continue doing my "love"—helping people through a radio program—without taking anything away from mothering. Yes, I was satisfied—and thankfully youthfully energetic enough to handle it all.

There is a danger, though, that when you take on extra responsibilities and activities, you will further add to your mental and physical exhaustion. As another SAHM put it,

> I find that the times when the whole house is stressed and cranky and nothing seems to be going well directly correspond to the times when I am spending more hours on the work or volunteering. I find that being a SAHM and the household

manager of my family is more than a full-time job.
I'm not saying you can't work from home, but my
experience has been that it's not that easy and has
consequences.

Back when I just had one baby, I had naptimes
to work, or I could do lots of things while she
played next to me. Now that doesn't work, since I
have three mobile, busy kids and have to deal with
getting them to and from school, to and from
activities, and then trying not to be working when
we are actually all at home together.

I figure I'll have time for those things again
when my youngest starts school, but right now
"work" is just another stress. I only say this be-
cause I think lots of women think, "Oh, I'll work
from home and bring in some money." It may not
work out with respect to time and energy.

Too many women actually believe that all the work
and effort that goes into being a SAHM isn't very
meaningful, specifically because they're not bringing
in money. Some have even called me to say they feel
guilt, as though they were idly living off somebody!
Good grief! Does that mean that the person who
tightens the last nut on the engine of a fighter jet has
no importance because he isn't flying the darn thing?

Let's see a pilot get a plane off the ground without that nut tightened! It is a team effort—just like a family. No one is more important just because he or she touches the money first—that's a sad, even disgusting, thought.

Whenever a woman tells me—ugh—that her husband has used making the money as his argument for having more power or importance in the family, I tell her to tell him that she's going to buy spiked heels and a large purse, become a high-priced call girl, and make more an hour than he does! That usually gets a laugh out of her, and a choked sound out of him.

One SAHM wrote,

> I personally know three women that did not go to college at all before raising their children. One woman started college the same day as the last of her five children did, and is now a successful marriage and family counselor with her own office and hours. Another raised five of her own and several foster children and adoptees, then purchased a women's gym and is working full-time. The third started college after raising four children and is now a nurse. These women are inspiring to me. Women can have it all—just not all at the same time.

MAKE IT FUN

Being a SAHM is the best and worst of all worlds. It is draining financially, emotionally, physically, and mentally. And if you're not careful, monotony can set in. You're drained from sunup to sundown and beyond with seemingly endless responsibilities that don't necessarily vary that much from day to day. But unlike most jobs, it is immediately rewarding, "even when you think at times you'll go crazy," wrote a SAHM.

> As far as getting through the day without going crazy . . . I do all kinds of projects with my kids. I'm not talking about sending the kids to soccer, and then to music lessons, and everything else in between. We do all kinds of projects making stuff from common household ingredients like paint, bubbles, dough, etc. My kids love to color with markers, crayons, and paint. We play outside, blow bubbles, read books, play puzzles. Sometimes something as simple as gluing macaroni onto paper will completely entertain my two-year-old.
>
> I find doing an activity will get my mind off of anything that might be bothering me at the time, and will usually entertain my little one so he's

ready for a nap when we're through. Then I get a moment to rest and regroup.

Cleaning and cooking on a daily basis can become a bit of a bore—like anything else, including a job at an office. The key is to find ways to make it a challenge—and to make it fun. I always thought cleaning while dancing was great—that's probably why I like the Swiffer commercials. I remember my mother polishing the floors—no, not on her hands and knees. Every day she would put a rag under each of her feet and glide through the house going about whatever activities, with the floor being polished along the way. I personally never minded folding and ironing because I would put an old movie on the television (*Captains Courageous*, for example) and work while sniffling over some sad scene. Yeah, even that can be fun!

I would make sure Deryk had access to activities wherever I was. My part-time work to make a few extra bucks was to teach machine knitting once a week. I had a shed out back, and students would come and take lessons. Deryk would sit on the floor and play, as most boys do, war scenarios with many of the knitting-machine parts. Or he would do artwork. He was there with me, having a ball and socializing with all the women.

The key, though, as that SAHM mentioned, is not to let activities and part-time work trump family time or your own health and sparkling personality. Remember, if you're becoming edgy, it's time to dump ballast.

Advice from one SAHM about enjoying this time of your life: "I would remind new SAHMs that time flies. With my first child I anticipated each stage and kept looking to the next. Now I cherish each stage and appreciate the curled-up little bundle of a newborn, the curiousness and happiness of a toddler, the newfound independence of school-age children . . . the specialness of each stage. I have found myself saying, 'This is the best stage!' about almost every stage my kids have been in."

Instead of trying to conquer your kids in their "stages," go to the place inside yourself where you make the effort to find things to cherish today as well as in your memory of yesterday. The fun comes in the passion of living; that passion can be squashed into oblivion by resentment and frustration. You actually have a decision in whether or not you're going to be happy. Happiness is not a viral infection over which you have no say or control. For the most part happiness is a choice you make; you know the saying about making lemonade out of lemons. When children grow up with a confident and happy mom, their whole world is a better place.

Perhaps you should make it a point, a goal, to be happy and put effort into that. How can I be happy with a kid with diarrhea? you may ask. Easy. Realize how wonderful it is for your child that you are there to keep her clean and warm, calm and loved, cared about and healed. The joy is not in the illness, of course; the joy is in the caretaking—how special and safe you've made your children feel, just by being you . . . and there with them.

WHEN YOU'RE "LOSING IT"

It won't hurt a child to cry for a while if you need to leave the room and get control of your emotions, but it may hurt them if you stay," warns one SAHM.

Everybody has a moment, hour, or time when they've "had it." Usually you can push yourself through it; sometimes you can't. When you can't, you need to be responsible, sensitive, and compassionate enough at that moment to stop yourself from escalating into screaming or hitting. This is when it's time to head for the bathroom and throw some water on your face; head for the telephone and call your mom or best girlfriend; contact your husband, let him know you're frazzled, and have him say some supportive somethings into your ear; stop what you're doing and change your scenery completely (go outside for a walk or take the kids for a ride to the park or mall); make yourself a cup of tea or coffee and have a one-cookie treat; or go into your bedroom for a bit and just have a good cry.

After a while you'll get good enough to sense way in advance when you're getting to that strung-out point, and you can head it off by doing the kinds of things you know cheer you up, or by not doing the kinds of things that are stressing you out. You need to gauge what you need to do so that you don't end up doing or saying something to your child or husband that will cause them—and you—deep pain and regret.

Sometimes you won't handle it right at all. Sometimes you will be a screaming, crazy ass. It happens. First thing you need to do is acknowledge it and take responsibility for letting yourself get too tired or frustrated by an unworkable schedule or set of expectations. Taking responsibility means you don't outright say, or give your husband and children the impression, that they are somehow at fault. Taking responsibility means you acknowledge that you just went OD and need something in order to get yourself back: a shower, walk, or talk. Always remember to apologize. It is amazing how understanding even children and harried husbands get when you admit to your weakness and faults and ask for their forgiveness. It gives children a great lesson in compassion and humanity and allows your husband to help you—which makes all men feel needed and useful.

One of the most touching things you can do to help yourself is to look at your kids' pictures often. "It pulls my perspective right back to where it should be very quickly. When I look at their baby pics, toddler pics, even ones just taken last year, all of a sudden the days seem so short, and the annoying things they do are endearing. I see how quickly their faces change and their interests change and their voices change . . . and suddenly I feel love and patience toward them," explained another SAHM.

The reason reviewing old photos works so well is that when you feel overwhelmed, it is as though the day, the moment you are in, just became magnified a thousand-fold, overwhelming your memory and your emotions. When you look at photos of those "cute" moments, the experience becomes spread over time, and lovely things are brought to mind—and heart.

Summary Thoughts

Nine years ago I left a job I loved and was good at. My bosses appreciated me and my work. Many of my former coworkers are still there. I'm sure they still think of me (fondly!) from time to time.

But to be honest, I was replaced in a matter of weeks, and I'm certain whoever took over my position was equally talented, brilliant, and responsible. The company got along fine without me all of these years.

However, my siblings and I lost our dear mom when she was only forty-seven. I miss her and think of her often. A mother holds a special place in your heart, and no one can take that place. I want to devote my time, energy, and talents where they count: creating memories for and with my children; teaching them, learning from them, laughing with them, playing with them, guiding them, loving them . . . and being loved in return.

Another SAHM wrote the following, which I think summarizes it all:

What would I recommend a woman do to prepare to be a SAHM? Well, learn how to go to sleep anywhere and at any time that you can. Read lots of books about potty training—it is still a mystery to me. Learn to ask the question "Is it critical?" before becoming upset, so you can pick your battles. The battles will come, but if you can choose when, where, and how to engage, you're more likely to win (any tactician could tell you that). If it isn't critical, maybe you can just let it go. Learn to relax. I let my first two kids stress me out so much because I tried to be perfect in everything and make them perfect too. No one's perfect. I'm happier since I learned to shrug and sigh. Learn to think outside the box; children are very creative, and sometimes you have to be creative to help them through their struggles or to get through to them. Oh, and buy a lot of Mr. Clean Magic Erasers when the kids are old enough for crayons.

Postscript

The day before I sat down to write this postscript, my twenty-two-year-old son called me in the middle of the day from his army base to tell me he had something very important to tell me, and I should listen carefully. Of course I freaked out instantly, certain there must be some really bad news for him to sound so sober.

He proceeded to tell me that there are only a few times in one's life that one feels comfortable saying the things that should always be said, but rarely are, and this was going to be one of those moments.

Yipes! What?

He then shared his feelings about me, past, present, and future. While what he said is quite personal and therefore private, let me just say that what he said touched me so deeply I couldn't breathe . . . it was just lovely.

Not having had a loving relationship with my two contentious parents, I've long reminded myself, and my listeners, that we have two opportunities for a quality parent-child relationship. The first we don't choose. The second we create.

God bless the second chance.

Did I miss out on anything by being a SAHM?

Are you kidding?

Blessings,

Dr. Laura

Dr. Laura Schlessinger

Post-Postscript

Mother Laura's Top Five Things
a Mom Needs to Do
to Be a Successful SAHM

1. Work with your husband to create a team spirit and joint effort that doesn't pit you both against each other with complaints, etc., but instead makes you both feel lovingly interdependent.

2. Make sure you spend time with and get support from women who share your values. Minimize your exposure to those who (out of their defensiveness) attempt to dismiss or diminish your home life and lifestyle.

3. Don't allow yourself to get into a rut, too focused on making sure all things are done and done perfectly. Allow fluidity in your day so that you

and your children may enjoy each other and life in general.

4. Don't let even one day pass without ticking off in your mind the joys and pleasures of that day . . . yes, in spite of the nonsense and annoyances that have also occurred. Make sure that when your husband comes home, you have only the former to tell him. That will make him excited about coming home to his family, and make you feel more satisfaction in your life.

5. Make sure that each and every day you tell your husband how much it means to you that he works to support you all, and that he is your hero.

Mother Laura's Top Five Things a Dad Needs to Do to Help His Wife Be the Best SAHM She Can Be

1. Make sure that you work diligently to provide for the family without fishing for compliments by complaining or bragging. It would be wonderful for you to tell your wife how good it makes you feel as a man to take care of her and the children.

2. Every night that you come home, find something to compliment about the home, children, or your wife—even if you are totally beat from your day. You will find that the act of complimenting seems to take that feeling of exhaustion out of your mind. Never nitpick about a little mess or an unironed shirt. None of that is more important than the love you have for her efforts to raise your children and take care of you and your nest.

3. Make sure that you find some time almost every day (early morning or late at night) to talk to

your wife as "your woman" or "your girlfriend," so that she always feels her femininity and sense of sensuality. Sex is part of this, but rubbing her feet, neck, or back also helps melt away the day's cares and reconnects her to you.

4. Take every public opportunity you can find to brag about your wife and kids in her presence. Show her how proud you are of her, and how appreciative you are for her creation of a home out of a house.

5. Make sure that you provide break or girl time for your wife, so she can recharge her emotional and physical batteries.

Finally: you should both spend your waking hours thinking of ways to make each other's lives more worth living.

Appendix:

Dr. Laura's Resources for Stay-at-Home Moms

Stay-at-Home Web Sites

Tips on shopping, crafts, forums, newsletters, support groups, and so on.

- Homebodies.org (features *Woman Power* on the home page)

- Amomsreview.com

- Baby-place.com

- Contestformoms.com

- Familyandhome.org

- Homewiththekids.com

- Kaboose.com

- Mainstreetmom.com

- Mommysavers.com

- Momsnetwork.com

- Mothersandmore.org

- Simplesahm.com

- Thenewhomemaker.com

- Womensforum.com

Recipes/Cooking

- Busymomsrecipes.com

- Familyfun.com/recipe

- Recipesformom.com

- Recipes.momsbreak.com

Coupons/Saving Money

- Couponmom.com

- Coupons.com

- Frugalliving.about.com

- Shopathome.com

- Stretcher.com

Budgets

- Budget5000.com

- Mint.com

- Planabudget.com

Organization

- Getorganizednow.com

- Help-organize-life.com

- Organizerightnow.com

Kids' Play/Games

- Creativekidsathome.com

- Funattic.com

- Gameskidsplay.net

- Kids-fun-and-games.com

Working from Home

- Homeworkingmom.com

- Jobsformoms.com

- Mommyenterprises.com (includes tips, parenting resources, and work-at-home jobs)

- Showmomthemoney.com

- Wahm.com

- Workathomechronicle.com

- Wwork.com

SAHM Book Resources

★ = Featured in our Reading Corner

Baird, Lori, and Rose Kennedy. *The Family Fitness Fun Book: Healthy Living for the Whole Family*. New York: Hatherleigh Press, 2005.

Burton, Linda, Janet Dittmer, and Cheri Loveless. *What's a Smart Woman Like You Doing at Home?* Rev. ed. Darby, PA: Mothers at Home, 1995.

★Corners, Christine. *From High Heels to Bunny Slippers: Surviving the Transition from Career to Home*. Sterling, VA: Capital Books, 2006.

Dacyczyn, Amy. *The Complete Tightwad Gazette.* New York: Villard, 1998.

*Dobson, Linda. *Homeschooling: The Early Years; Your Complete Guide to Successfully Homeschooling the 3- to 8-Year-Old Child.* New York: Three Rivers Press, 1999.

*Eberly, Sheryl. *365 Manners Kids Should Know: Games, Activities, and Other Fun Ways to Help Children Learn Etiquette.* New York: Three Rivers Press, 2001.

*Economides, Steve, and Annette Economides. *America's Cheapest Family Gets You Right on the Money.* New York: Three Rivers Press, 2007.

*Edwards, Paul. *Working from Home.* 5th ed. New York: Tarcher, 1999.

Elkind, David. *The Power of Play: Learning What Comes Naturally.* Cambridge, MA: Da Capo Press, 2007.

*Ely, Leanne. *Healthy Foods: An Irreverent Guide to Understanding Nutrition and Feeding Your Family Well.* Vancouver, WA: Champion Press, 2001.

*English, Andrea. *Million Dollar Mom: No Sweepstakes Necessary to Be a Stay-at-Home Mom.* Mustang, OK: Tate, 2006.

*Ettus, Samantha. *The Experts' Guide to Life at Home.* New York: Clarkson Potter, 2005.

Evers, Connie Liakos. *How to Teach Nutrition to Kids.* 3rd ed. Vancouver, BC: 24 Carrot Press, 2006.

*Flanagan, Caitlin. *To Hell with All That: Loving and Loathing Our Inner Housewife.* New York: Back Bay Books, 2007.

*Fliegel, Catherine. *The One-Armed Cook: Quick and Easy Recipes, Smart Meal Plans, and Savvy Advice for New (and Not-So-New) Moms.* Des Moines, IA: Meredith Books, 2005.

Fox, Isabelle, and Norman M. Lobsenz. *Being There: The Benefits of a Stay-at-Home Parent.* Hauppauge, NY: Barrons, 1996.

*Gavin, Mary L. *Fit Kids: A Practical Guide to Raising Active and Healthy Children—From Birth to Teens.* New York: DK, 2004.

Gochnauer, Cheryl. *So You Want to Be a Stay-at-Home Mom.* Downers Grove, IL: InterVarsity Press, 1999.

———. *Stay-at-Home Handbook.* Downers Grove, IL: InterVarsity Press, 2002.

Goulet, Mary, and Heather Reider. *The Momstown Guide to Getting It All: A Life Makeover for Stay-at-Home Moms.* New York: Hyperion, 2005.

*Griffin, Glen C. *It Takes a Parent to Raise a Child.* New York: St. Martin's Press, 2000.

*Hamman, Rachel. *Bye-Bye Boardroom: Confessions from a New Breed of Stay-at-Home Moms.* Sterling, VA: Capital Books, 2006.

*Hunt, Gladys. *Honey for a Child's Heart: The Imaginative Use of Books in Family Life.* New York: Harper-Collins, 2002.

*Hunter, Brenda. *Home by Choice: Raising Emotionally Secure Children in an Insecure World.* Phoenix, AZ: Multnomah Books, 2006.

Jones, Katina K. *The 200 Best Home Businesses: Easy to Start, Fun to Run, Highly Profitable.* 2nd ed. Cincinnati: Adams Media, 2005.

*Kellam, Tawra Jean. *Not Just Beans: 50 Years of Frugal Family Favorites.* 2nd ed. Not Just Beans Publishing, 2002.

*Kellam, Tawra Jean, and Jill Cooper. *Dining on a Dime Cook Book: 1000 Money Saving Recipes and Tips.* Newtown Square, PA: Newman Marketing, 2004.

*Kohl, Susan Isaacs. *The Best Things Parents Do.* Newburyport, MA: Conari Press, 2004.

Kuffner, Trish. *The Toddlers Busy Book.* Minnetonka, MN: Meadowbrook Press, 1999.

*Lee, Jeffrey. *Catch a Fish, Throw a Ball, Fly a Kite: 21 Timeless Skills Every Child Should Know (and Any Parent Can Teach!).* New York: Three Rivers Press, 2004.

Nicholas-Gervais, Vera. *Time Out: Soul Talk for Stay-at-Home Moms.* Montreal: Soulgoals Press, 2002.

Peters, Angie. *Celebrate Home: Great Ideas for Stay-at-Home Moms.* Springtown, TX: Arch Books, 2005.

Robertson, Brian C. *There's No Place Like Work: How Business, Government, and Our Obsession with Work Have Driven Parents from Home.* Dallas: Spence, 2000.

Sachs, Wendy. *How She Really Does It: Secrets of Success from Stay-at-Work Moms.* New York: Perseus, 2006.

Sanders, Darcie. *Staying Home: From Full-Time Professional to Full-Time Parent.* Boston: Little, Brown, 1992.

Singer, Jen. *14 Hours 'Til Bedtime: A Stay-at-Home Mom's Life in 27 Funny Little Stories.* 2nd ed. Deadwood, OR: Wyatt-MacKenzie, 2005.

Stanton, Melissa. *The Stay-at-Home Survival Guide: Field-Tested Strategies for Staying Smart, Sane, and Connected While Caring for Your Kids.* Berkeley, CA: Seal Press, 2008.

*Steede-Terry, Karen. *Full-Time Woman, Part-Time Career.* Cedar Park, TX: CMS Press, 2005.

Stone, Pamela. *Opting Out? Why Women Really Quit Careers and Head Home.* Berkeley and Los Angeles: University of California Press, 2008.

*Tamsevicius, Kristie. *I Love My Life: A Mom's Guide to Working from Home.* Deadwood, OR: Wyatt-MacKenzie, 2003.

*Taylor-Hough, Deborah. *Frozen Assets: How to Cook for a Day and Eat for a Month.* Vancouver, WA: Champion Press, 1998.

Tinglof, Christina Baglivi. *The Organized Parent: 365 Simple Solutions to Managing Your Home, Your Time, and Your Family's Life.* New York: McGraw-Hill, 2002.

*Tolliver, Cindy. *At-Home Motherhood: Making It Work for You.* San Jose, CA: Resource, 1994.

*Venker, Suzanne. *7 Myths of Working Mothers: Why Children and (Most) Careers Just Don't Mix.* Dallas: Spence, 2004.

*Walker, Christine. *The Smart Mom's Guide to Staying Home: 65 Simple Ways to Thrive, Not Deprive, on One Income.* Victoria, BC: Trafford, 2006.

*White, Burton L. *Raising a Happy, Unspoiled Child.* New York: Fireside, 1995.

*Wolk, Claudine. *It Gets Easier! . . . And Other Lies We Tell New Mothers!* Doylestown, PA: New Buck Press, 2008.

Wyckoff, Malia McCawley, and Mary Snyder. *You Can Afford to Stay Home with Your Kids: A Step-by-Step Guide for Converting Your Family from Two Incomes to One.* Franklin Lakes, NJ: Career Press, 1999.